The Philosopher's Dictionary

The Philosopher's Dictionary

by

Robert M. Martin

broadview press

Cataloguing in Publication Data

Martin, Robert M.
    The philosopher's dictionary

ISBN 0-921149-75-1

1.. Philosophy — Dictionaries   I. Title.

    B41.M37 1991   103   C91–093624–2

broadview press   in the US, broadview press
P.O. Box 1243   269 Portage Rd.
Peterborough, Ontario   Lewiston, NY
K9J 7H5   Canada   14092   USA

in the UK: c/o Drake Marketing Services, Market
Pl., Deddington, Oxfordshire OX15 OSF

Printed in Canada

To Fran, who loves five-dollar words

ABOUT THIS DICTIONARY

PHILOSOPHERS HAVE THEIR OWN technical vocabulary —
perhaps more of it than in any other academic field — and
often use ordinary words in special ways. Thus this dictionary. I have tried to locate terms in here where you'd likely
look for them first, but there is a great deal of cross-refer-
ence, in case you look somewhere else. Alphabetization ig-
nores spaces and punctuation. Phrases are defined in
entries alphabetized according to the real order of the
words: for example, there is an entry defining 'general will'
among the G's, cross-referenced under 'will, general'
among the W's. Contrasting or very closely related terms
are defined together: thus 'analytic' and 'synthetic' are both
defined in the entry for 'analytic / synthetic', to which the
entry for 'synthetic' will refer you. Slashes are used to
separate such related terms.

Before the modern era, people were formally referred to
often by their first names. So, for example, the entry for
'Thomas Aquinas' is alphabetized under the T's (though
cross-referenced under the A's). I have often given
philosophers' full names when they are commonly referred
to only by a shorter name. Parentheses tell you what to
leave out when mentioning them. For example, J(ohn)
L(angshaw) Austin is almost always called J. L. Austin, and
we talk of Auguste Comte, not (Isadore) Auguste (Marie
François) Comte.

Some definitions use words I define elsewhere; where it might be helpful for you to look up these words, they are in SMALL CAPITALS. For brevity I ignore obvious grammatical variations (for example, 'CONSISTENT' in one definition refers the reader to the entry under 'consistency'). When a term inside a definition is defined elsewhere, but not under its own heading, the entry in which it is defined is noted in a 'See ...' comment. I note related terms which it might be helpful for you to consult in a 'See also ...' comment.

I have given spelling variations, warnings about common misspellings, usage directions, and pronunciations, where useful in square brackets. When it would be uncommon, or pretentious, or very difficult for English speakers to use the original pronunciation of words or names that come from other languages, I have given the best acceptable English (mis)pronunciation. (I ignore the French 'r' and nasalized vowels, for example; but pronounce them if you can.)

There is a Greek or Latin name associated with almost every philosophical concept talked about before 1600, and there is a non-English word for many concepts associated with non-English-speaking philosophers. I have included non-English words when they are likely to be found un-translated in English philosophical writing. The non-English terms are in italics, though most of them have been naturalized into working philosophical English and need not be underlined or italicized in your writing. Some Greek and Latin words have a line over a vowel (example: 'agapē'); this mark is optional in English writing.

To keep this book short enough to be handy, I have kept definitions brief and basic. There is much more to be said! A useful (but cumbersome) reference work, far longer and more detailed than this, is *The Encyclopedia of Philosophy* (New York: Macmillan, 1967). And, of course, there's no substitute for reading philosophical works themselves.

I hope that you'll find this book friendly, informal, and helpful. My aim has been to give definitions that can be understood by people who don't already know what the defined term means. (Surprisingly, other philosophical dictionaries don't seem to have been written with this in mind!) I have tried to include all the basic philosophical words, and to be even-handed; but this book must reflect my own philosophical biases and training. If you find unhelpful definitions, or important words left out, or implicit philosophical bias, please write me at the Philosophy Department, Dalhousie University, Halifax, Nova Scotia, Canada B3H 3J5. Your suggestions will be gratefully acknowledged, and will be considered for future revised editions.

I have several people to thank for their great help: the anonymous readers for Broadview Press, and (in alphabetical order) David Braybrooke, Steven Burns, Doug Butler, Rich Campbell, Mary MacLeod, Roland Puccetti, Tom Vinci, Sheldon Wein, and Anna Zaniewska.

I love words but I don't like strange ones.
You don't understand them and they don't
understand you.

Will Rogers

feather: 1a: one of the light horny
epidermal outgrowths that form the
external covering of the body of birds and
that consist of a shaft bearing on each side
a series of barbs which bear barbules
which in turn bear barbicels commonly
ending in hooked hamuli and interlocking
with the barbules of an adjacent barb to
link the barbs into a continuous vane.

Webster's Seventh New Collegiate Dictionary

A

Abélard, Peter (or Pierre) (1079-1142) French philosopher with works mainly on THEOLOGY, LOGIC, METAPHYSICS, and ethics. Noted for his position on UNIVERSALS: he argued that only INDIVIDUALS exist, and that general terms stand for ABSTRACTIONS of the mind.

absolute 'Absolute' as used in philosophy often means 'complete, perfect, independent, unchanging, not RELATIVE'. Some philosophers think that something called 'the absolute' exists, basic to the EXPLANATION of other things; but perhaps this is only a REIFICATION. HEGEL identified the absolute spirit with God, and thought that it manifests itself in developments in the world (*see* HISTORICAL MATERIALISM / IDEALISM). Other philosophers associated with this term are SCHELLING and BRADLEY. Sometimes capitalized: 'the Absolute'; 'Absolute Spirit'.

absolute space and time The view that space and time exist independently of the objects and events in them. This was Newton's view, rejected by Einstein, among others (*See* SCIENTISTS).

absolutism, ethical / cultural *See* RELATIVISM / ABSOLUTISM.

abstraction An abstraction is a general sort of thing, as opposed to a particular (*See* INDIVIDUALS) — for example, greenness, as distinguished from any and all particular green things. It seems that abstractions aren't directly perceived; we can see particular green things, and see that each is green, but we can't see greenness itself. Perhaps greenness is known by the process of abstraction—i.e., as the result of thinking about green things—or perhaps (as PLATO and others have argued) we must have independent prior knowledge of greenness in order to be able to classify the particulars (*see* PLATONIC FORMS). The question whether abstract things exist is one way of putting the problem of UNIVERSALS. (*See also* CONCEPT).

absurdity 1. Something clearly false or SELF-CONTRADICTORY. Deriving an absurdity in this sense from the denial of what is to be proved is what happens in a *reductio ad absurdum* — an INDIRECT PROOF. **2.** Something unreasonable, meaningless, inappropriate, without structure, incoherent, failing to make sense. EXISTENTIALISTS hold that reality, and our place in it, are absurd in this sense.

Academy *The Akadēmia* (Greek: "Academy") was the place in Athens where PLATO taught. Thus, the word came to refer to the disciples of Plato, the PLATONISTS, and more generally (with a lower-case 'a'), to any association of scholars (whence the term 'academic'). Don't be too hasty to dismiss some point as "purely academic" if you are in an academy.

access, privileged *See* PRIVILEGED ACCESS.

accident *See* ESSENCE / ACCIDENT.

accidental quality / characteristic *See* ESSENCE / ACCIDENT.

Achilles and the tortoise *See* ZENO'S PARADOX.

acquaintance, knowledge by *See* KNOWLEDGE BY ACQUAINTANCE / BY DESCRIPTION.

act / agent moralities Some moral philosophers think that the basic sort of thing ethics evaluates is the worth of ACTIONS people do (act morality); others think that what's basic to moral theory is the person who acts (AGENT morality). KANT argued that good actions were those done by people with the right sort of motives, so his ethical theory is a variety of agent morality; the UTILITARIANS thought that the basic kind of ethical thought evaluates actions, whatever the motives or moral worth of the people who do them, so their ethics is a variety of act morality.

action A human action is distinguished from just any bodily movement, usually on the basis that an action must be intended. Thus your accidentally spilling your coffee is not an action; neither is the motion of your tongue while you drink your coffee, because you do not think about that motion, or intend that it be the way it is. ('Act' is used in the same way.)

action-at-a-distance The effect that one thing can have on another that it is not touching and to which it is not connected by something in-between. Gravitation is an example. Some philosophers and scientists — e.g., LEIBNIZ — thought that this was impossible. One way they tried to explain gravitation is to suppose that bodies that gravitationally attract each other are connected by some intervening invisible thing that fills the space between them, and transfers the gravitational force.

action theory The branch of philosophy that considers questions about ACTION. Examples of these are: What differentiates an action from other movements? Can there be actions that are refrainings from acting? Where does an action end and its consequences begin? Moral questions (about, for example, ACTS / OMISSIONS) and the questions of FREE WILL and responsibility are sometimes included in action theory.

active euthanasia *See* EUTHANASIA, ACTIVE / PASSIVE.

acts / ommissions An act is doing something, by contrast with an omission (or refraining), which is merely failing to do something. Some philosophers think that there can be a moral difference between these even when they have the same outcome. For example, it has been argued that an act of killing someone is worse than merely refraining from saving someone's life, even when they have exactly the same motives and results.

acts, speech *See* SPEECH ACTS.

act utilitarianism *See* UTILITARIANISM.

ad baculum (Latin: "[appeal] to force") An illogical means of persuasion in which one attempts to convince not by giving reasons that provide genuine logical support, but by threatening. Example: "Druid non-Euclidianism has the only correct philosophical view on this matter. If you don't think so, wait to see what mark I give you on the next exam." One of the informal FALLACIES. ['ad BAK-you-lum']

ad hoc (Latin: "to this" i.e., "specially for this purpose") An *ad hoc* ASSUMPTION is one that is introduced illicitly in an attempt to save some position from a contrary ARGUMENT or COUNTER EXAMPLE intended to show that the position is false. It is illicit because it is designed especially to accommodate the argument or counter example, and has no independent support. One of the informal FALLACIES. An example of *ad hoc* reasoning (adapted from St. AUGUSTINE):

"Suicide is always wrong."

"Well, how about all those women who in early Christian times killed themselves rather than being raped by pagan soldiers, and whom you count as saints?"

"That doesn't show that suicide is permissible. In those cases, they must have been acting under direct secret orders from God, so what they did was OK."

ad hominem (Latin: "to the person") A logically mistaken (but sometimes persuasive) form of ARGUMENT in which, instead of giving good reasons against some position, one irrelevantly attacks or abuses the person who held that position. An example: "Plato's theory of forms can't be correct because Plato was a known, practising homosexual." One of the informal FALLACIES. ['ad' + 'HAH-ma-nem' or 'HOH-mee-nem']

ad ignorantium (Latin: "to ignorance") A logically mistaken (but sometimes persuasive) form of ARGUMENT in which one argues for some position by claiming that nobody can show that it's false (or that a position is false because no one can prove that it is true). Example: "God must exist, because it's impossible to give any definite disproof of His existence." One of the informal FALLACIES. ['ad' + 'ig-na-RANT-ee-um' or 'ig'na'RANCE-ee-um']

A / E / I / O propositions This distinction among kinds of statements, used in TRADITIONAL LOGIC, is best explained by examples:

A: All pigs are mammals.

E: No pigs are mammals.

I: Some pigs are mammals.

O: Some pigs are not mammals.

aesthetics The philosophical study of art, of our reactions to it, and of similar reactions to things that are not works of art. Typical questions here are: What is the definition of 'art'? How can we judge aesthetic worth? Is this an objective matter? ['ass-' or 'es' + 'THET-iks'; sometimes (especially in the U.S.) spelled 'esthetics']

aether *See* ETHER.

aetiology The study of the causes of something or some sort of thing. ['ee-tee-AH-lo-jee'; sometimes (especially in the U.S.) spelled 'etiology']

affirming the consequent An incorrect mode of reasoning involving the CONDITIONAL, in which one derives the antecedent from a conditional plus its consequent. Example:

If it rained this morning, the pavement would be wet now.

The pavement is wet.

Therefore it must have rained this morning.

a fortiori (Latin: "from what is stronger") With even stronger reason. "Killing even one innocent person is wrong, so Hitler's actions are, *a fortiori*, immoral." [usually 'ay FOR-she-OR-ee', sometimes 'ah FOR-tee-OR-ee']

agapē (Greek: "love") In Christian philosophy, Christian love, including our love of God and His of us; also refers to a Christian ceremony of worship and fondness of the worshippers for each other. Sometimes contrasted with *eros* (passionate or erotic love; for the PLATONISTS, the love of the eternal perfect PLATONIC FORMS, such as truth and beauty) and with *philia* (brotherly love, fondness, or friendship). ['AH-ga-pee']

agathon / aretē The first is a Greek adjective associated with the second a Greek noun. 'Arete' is ordinarily translated as 'VIRTUE', with the association of excellence and fulfilment of function and potential; thus, '*agathon*' is for the Greeks a term of praise: 'good'. ['AH-reh-tee']

agreement, method of *See* MILL'S METHODS.

agent The person who does an ACTION.

agent causation Often it is thought that causes and effects must be events—for example, human actions and decisions. This leads to problems (*see* FREE WILL and DETERMINISM). In response to these problems, some philosophers have claimed that the cause of our actions is not a (determined) event (such as a decision), but rather an AGENT (the person who acts); this is supposed to get around these problems.

agent moralities *See* ACT / AGENT MORALITIES.

agnosticism *See* ATHEISM / THEISM / AGNOSTICISM.

AI *See* ARTIFICIAL INTELLIGENCE.

akrasia (Greek: "bad mixture," "lacking in self control or moderation") The character trait in one who knows what is right to do but doesn't do it; weakness of will. This notion is puzzling: doesn't one always do what one really, overall, thinks best? For similar puzzles, *see* BURIDAN'S ASS and SELF-DECEPTION. ['ah-kra-SEE-ah' or 'uh-KRAY-zha']

Albertus Magnus, St. (or Albert the Great; original name Albert, Count von Bellstädt) (1206?-1280) German SCHOLASTIC philosopher and theologian, known for his efforts to combine Greek, Arabic, and Christian thought; teacher of THOMAS AQUINAS.

alethic Means 'having to do with necessity and possibility'. Alethic logic is that branch of MODAL LOGIC concerned with the connections between sentences involving 'necessary', 'possible', 'impossible', etc. 'It's necessary that P' is often symbolized '$\Box$P'; and 'it's possible that P' as '$\Diamond$P'. ['ah-LEE-thick']

al-Fārābī *See* Fārābī, Al-.

algorithm A mechanical method (i.e., one determined by strict rules, needing no creativity or ingenuity to apply) for carrying out a given calculation in a finite number of steps.

alienation Estrangement, separation. The EXISTENTIALISTS thought that an important and inevitable part of the human condition was our alienation from nature and from each other. In MARX, 'alienation' means the separation from the products of our labour (as employees, we don't own what we produce) as well as from society and from ourselves.

altruism 1. Generosity. **2.** The philosophical position that one ought to act for the benefit of others (*See also* EGOISM).

Althusser, Louis (b. 1918) French philosopher associated with the STRUCTURALISTS, known for his application of that theory to MARXIST thought.

ambiguity *See* EQUIVOCATION.

amorality *See* IMMORALITY / AMORALITY.

ampersand The symbol '&', meaning 'and'. *See* SYMBOLS OF SENTENTIAL LOGIC.

amphiboly A statement whose meaning is unclear because of its ambiguous grammatical construction. For example, 'If the Dodgers were playing the Yankees, I would root for them.' For whom? Also the name of the informal FALLACY that arises because of this ambiguity. ['am-FIB-oh-lee']

analogy / disanalogy An analogy is a similarity of two things. Reasoning from (or by) analogy is concluding that because two things share one or more characteristics, they share another. For example, some philosophers think they can solve the PROBLEM OF OTHER MINDS by analogy: other people share my general outward appearance and behaviour, so that's evidence that they also have minds. (This argument is associated with DESCARTES.) A disanalogy is a difference between compared things; disanalogies between things reduce the strength of an argument from analogy.

analysis Some things are capable of being understood in terms of their component (sometimes conceptual) parts; analysis takes them apart into their simpler elements. Reductive analysis aims to show that what is analyzed does not constitute a basic existent — or need not be thought of as existing at all (*see* REDUCTIONISM). Something to be analyzed is called the 'analysandum', and what provides the analysis is called the 'analysans'. *See also* ANALYTIC PHILOSOPHY.

analysis, linguistic *See* ANALYTIC PHILOSOPHY.

analytical behaviourism *See* BEHAVIOURISM.

analyticity *See* ANALYTIC / SYNTHETIC.

analytic philosophy A major tradition in philosophy, associated especially with the English-speaking philosophers; contrasted with speculative or CONTINENTAL philosophy. The distinction arose during the first few decades of the twentieth century when English philosophers (including RUSSELL and MOORE) revolted against the dominant HEGELIAN school. Analytic philosophers were so-called because they thought that a major part of philosophy is the ANALYSIS of CONCEPTS. Because of their frequent emphasis on language, this school is sometimes called 'linguistic philosophy' or 'linguistic analysis'. Impressed by the methods of science, they tended to think that philosophers had no business making substantive claims that are not VERIFIABLE. Nowadays both the analytic and the continental traditions include such a broad variety of approaches that these distinctions aren't very precise. These names tend mostly to be used as derogatory epithets for the competition. Contemporary analytic philosophers — roughly speaking — are those who have been influenced by EMPIRICISM, PRAGMATISM, and LOGICAL POSITIVISM, though few contemporary analytic philosophers accept all the basic tenets or methodologies of any of these positions.

analytic / synthetic These words were introduced by KANT, referring to the difference between two kinds of JUDGEMENT. Kant called a judgement analytic when the "PREDICATE was contained in the subject"; thus, for example, the judgement that all bachelors are unmarried is analytic because the subject ('bachelors') "contains" the predicate ('unmarried'). This possibly makes the notion the same as that of CONCEPTUAL TRUTH. Most philosophers think that this distinction is better made in terms of sentences: a sentence is analytic when the meaning of the subject of that sentence contains the meaning of the predicate: 'unmarried' is part of the definition of 'bachelor'. In other words, an analytic sentence is one that is true merely because of the meanings of the words. 'It's snowing or it's not snowing' is true merely because of the meaning of the words 'or' and 'not', so perhaps we should count this as analytic too. But since the relevant words in this case are *"logical"* words, this sentence is more particularly known as a LOGICAL TRUTH. A synthetic truth is a sentence that is true, but not merely because of the meaning of the words. 'Pigs don't fly' is true *partially* because of the meaning of the words, of course: if 'pigs' meant 'woodpeckers', then that sentence would be false. But since the definition of 'pig' tells us nothing about flying, this sentence is not true merely because of the meaning of the words. One can speak also about analytically false sentences, for example, 'There exists a married bachelor'. Be careful to distinguish among the analytic / synthetic, LOGICAL TRUTH / FALSITY, NECESSARY / CONTINGENT, and A PRIORI / A POSTERIORI. For example, analytic sentences are necessarily true, and may (sometimes) be known *a priori*; but there may also be synthetic a priori statements (Kant thought there were). QUINE argued that the analytic / synthetic distinction is not a good one, because one cannot distinguish between matters of meaning of the words of a sentence and matters of fact.

anarchism The view that government has no right to coerce citizens, that the best society is one with the least government, or with no government at all. A well-known advocate of philosophical anarchism is PROUDHON.

Anaxagoras (500?-?428 B.C.) PRE-SOCRATIC Greek METAPHYSICIAN and COSMOLOGIST. His writings contain speculations on the origins of the universe and the constituents of matter. ['an-ak-SAG-uh-rus']

Anaximander (c. 610-c. 546 B.C.) PRE-SOCRATIC Greek scientist and METAPHYSICIAN. Believed in a single SUBSTANCE (called "the indefinite") out of which everything was formed. ['uh-NAX-uh-man-der']

Anaximenes (d. c. 528 B.C.) PRE-SOCRATIC Greek METAPHYSICIAN and COSMOLOGIST. His candidate for the single SUBSTANCE that composed all existence was air (or mist). ['an-ax-IH-muh-neez']

ancient philosophy Ancient philosophy began in primitive form, we suppose, in prehistory; the earliest Western philosopher of whose work we have a historical account is THALES (c. 500 B.C.). The end of this period is often marked by the beginning of MEDIEVAL PHILOSOPHY, with the work of St. AUGUSTINE (about A.D. 400).

anguish *See* EXISTENTIAL ANGUISH.

anhedonia The state of being without happiness or pleasure. ['an-he-DOAN-i-a']

animism The view that things not normally thought to be so are alive, or at least are understandable in terms of features normally associated only with living things. This is usually associated with primitive religion, but a recent animistic view in science is the Gaia hypothesis—that the earth is (or is in some ways like) a living organism. *See also* ANTHROPOMORPHISM.

Anselm, St. (1033-1109) Italian-born, English SCHOLAS-
TIC theologian / philosopher, Archbishop of Canterbury.
An important philosopher of the early middle ages;
known for his defense of rational THEOLOGY and the
ONTOLOGICAL ARGUMENT FOR GOD'S EXISTENCE.

antecedent conditions The events or states of affairs
that come before a given event and that cause it, or are
necessary or sufficient (*See* NECESSARY / SUFFICIENT
CONDITIONS) for it to happen.

antecedent / consequent *See* CONDITIONAL.

anthropocentrism *See* SPECISM.

anthropomorphic Having human form, or human-like.
PRIMITIVE thought, for example, anthropomorphized
nature, seeing it as characterized by aims, emotions and
desires (for instance, seeing a thunderstorm as a
manifestation of anger). Some religious thought con-
ceives of God anthropomorphically, in that God is
thought of as having human desires and aims. ['AN-
throw-po-MOR-fick']

antinomy *See* PARADOX.

antirealism *See* REALISM / ANTIREALISM.

antithesis *See* DIALECTIC.

apodictic / assertoric / problematic 1. Apodictic
(sometimes spelled 'apodeictic') statements assert that
something must be the case; assertoric that something is
the case; problematic that something may be the case. **2.**
An apodictic statement is one that is clearly proven or
INDUBITABLE.

Apollonian / Dionysian NIETZSCHE distinguished these two sorts of approaches to art and, more generally, to life. The former tends toward order, rationality, harmony, clarity, and intellect; the latter toward disorder, spontaneity, imagination, energy, and creativity. Nietzsche associated Dionysian attitudes with the WILL TO POWER.

a posteriori *See* A PRIORI / A POSTERIORI.

appearance / reality The difference between the way things seem to us and the way they really are. Philosophers have often been concerned with this difference—with how to tell when (if ever) the way things appear is how they are.

a priori / a posteriori (Latin, "from before / from after") Two different ways in which something might be known to be true (or false). It can be known a priori if it can be known before, or independently of, sense-experience of the fact in question. It can be known a posteriori if it can be known on the basis of, after, sense-experience of the fact. One can know that all bachelors are unmarried a priori; one doesn't need to observe even one bachelor to know this is true. In this case (but perhaps not in all cases) a priori knowledge is possible because what's known is a CONCEPTUAL TRUTH or because the sentence that expresses this truth is ANALYTIC or LOGICALLY TRUE. The terms are associated with KANT, who argued that certain a priori truths were not conceptual or analytic, for example, that every event has a cause. A priori truths are sometimes called 'truths of reason'. ['ay' or 'ah' + 'pre-OR-ee' / 'pos-tee-ree-OR-ee']

a priori **probability** *See* PROBABILITY.

Aquinas, St. Thomas *See* THOMAS AQUINAS.

archē (Greek: "beginning" or "origin") The word was extended to mean 'principle' or 'foundation', and thus to refer to the basis of political authority, existence, or knowledge. ['AR-kay]

aretē *See* AGATHON / ARETE.

argument An argument in ordinary talk is a debate, especially a heated one. But in philosophical usage, an argument is one or more statements (called 'premises'; singular 'premise' or 'premiss') advanced in order to support another statement (the conclusion). Thus philosophers need not get angry when they argue. Premises actually support a conclusion only when there is the appropriate sort of logical connection between the premises and the conclusion. In DEDUCTIVE arguments, the conclusion must be true given the truth of the premises; in an INDUCTIVE argument, the truth of the premises makes the conclusion more probable. Any deductive argument in which the premises really do have the appropriate logical connection with the conclusion is called a 'valid' argument; in invalid arguments, this connection is lacking. A valid argument may, however, fail to support its conclusion because one or more of its premises is false — for example:

All pigs fly.

All flying things are lighter than air.

Therefore all pigs are lighter than air.

This argument is valid, but it fails to convince because both of its premises are false. An argument with at least one false premise is called 'unsound'; a sound argument is a valid argument all of whose premises are true. A sound argument provides a proof of its conclusion (though in logic it's often said that a proof is provided merely when the argument is valid). [The word 'argument' is sometimes misspelled by students: please note that it is not spelled 'arguement'.]

argument from analogy *See* ANALOGY.

argument from design *See* TELEOLOGICAL ARGUMENT.

argument of a function *See* FUNCTION.

arguments for God's existence —*See* the following well-known ones: COMMON CONSENT ARGUMENT, DEGREES OF PERFECTION ARGUMENT, FIRST CAUSE ARGUMENT, MORAL ARGUMENT, MYSTICAL EXPERIENCE ARGUMENT, ONTOLOGICAL ARGUMENT, PASCAL'S WAGER, TELEOLOGICAL ARGUMENT.

argument from illusion The argument (against NAIVE REALISM) that the existence of perceptual ILLUSIONS and hallucinations shows that we really directly perceive only SENSE-DATA and not an independent world.

argument, open question *See* OPEN QUESTION ARGUMENT.

Aristippus (435?-?356 B.C.) Greek SOPHIST, founder of the CYRENAIC school; follower of SOCRATES, known for his HEDONISTIC ethics. ['ar-is-TIP-us']

Aristotle (384-322 B.C.) Hugely influential Greek philosopher and scientist; some think the greatest philosopher. He was PLATO'S student; like his teacher, he was centrally concerned with knowledge of reality and of the right way to live. Unlike Plato, however, he accepted the reality of the EMPIRICAL, changing world, and attempted to discover what sort of understanding we must have in order to have knowledge of it. He argued that INDIVIDUAL things must be seen as belonging to kinds of things, each of which has ESSENTIAL properties that give it potential for change and development. (For Aristotle's distinction of kinds of properties, *see* EFFICIENT / FORMAL / MATERIAL / FINAL CAUSES.) Investigation into the essential properties of humans can tell us what human good is: he conceived it as a life lived in accord with the moral and intellectual VIRTUES. Aristotle's writings cover all sorts of areas in natural science and philosophy. He began the systematic study of LOGIC.

Arrow's theorem *See* VOTER'S PARADOX 2.

art 1. The process and the product involved in painting, sculpture, etc. (*See also* AESTHETICS.) **2.** Also, in a wider sense, in any intentional creation (or "artifact"). **3.** A 'term of art' (also called 'technical term') is thus a term used in a special, invented, technical way. Looking at this dictionary will show you that philosophy is full of terms of art.

artificial intelligence An area of study in computer science and psychology that involves building (or imagining) machines, or programming computers, to mimic certain complex intelligent human activities. The creation of a program that can play chess at a high level is one of its successes. Artificial intelligence is of philosophical interest insofar as it might shed light on what human mentality is like, and insofar as its successes and failures enter into arguments about MATERIALISM. [sometimes abbreviated 'AI']

artificial / natural language A natural language is one used by some actual group of people, that has developed on its own, culturally and historically. An artificial language is one developed for some purpose. Philosophers use the term to refer especially to IDEAL LANGUAGES. Computer languages are artificial language; SYMBOLIC LOGIC provides other examples.

asceticism The practice of living under extremely simple conditions, with minimal enjoyment, pleasure, and comfort. Sometimes ascetics even intentionally produce pain or discomfort. Certain religious enthusiasts thought this was a good idea. St. AUGUSTINE and SCHOPENHAUER gave philosophical arguments in favour of certain forms of asceticism. ['ah-SET-a-sism']

assertion A statement or sentence used to state a fact, to make a claim, true or false, about the way things are; or the act of saying or writing such a sentence. Distinguished from other sentences or acts that express feelings, ask questions, etc.: these sentences are neither true nor false. An indicative sentence that does not state anything that is true or false ('Tuesdays more than twelve pounds long juggle deeply') may be poetic, but isn't an assertion.

assertion sign *See* SYMBOLS OF SENTENTIAL LOGIC.

assertoric *See* APODEICTIC / ASSERTORIC / PROBLEMATIC.

asssumption 1. Something taken to be true, without argument or justification. **2.** = premise (*see* ARGUMENT.

asymmetric *See* SYMMETRIC / ASYMMETRIC / NONSYMMETRIC.

atheism / theism / agnosticism Atheism is the view that God does not exist. People who have never given a thought to the matter aren't called 'atheists' — the word is used only for people who believe there isn't any God.

Atheists sometimes (but not always) in addition think that religious practice is foolish, or that the morality fostered by religion is wrong. Because atheism has been, at times, so unpopular, atheistic philosophers have sometimes disguised their views. LUCRETIUS and HUME were probably atheists. RUSSELL, another famous atheist, was open about it (and got into trouble). Not every religion includes the belief in God — Buddhism, for example, is sometimes said to be an atheistic religion. Atheism is contrasted with its opposite, theism, the view that God does exist, and also with agnosticism, the view that there isn't any good reason to believe either that God exists or that He doesn't. [Note the way 'atheist', 'atheism', 'theist', and 'theism' are spelled: 'e' before 'i'.]

atomic facts / propositions *See* LOGICAL ATOMISM.

atomism The view that things are composed of elementary basic parts. From ancient times till the present, physics was often atomistic (though what's now called an 'atom' is no longer regarded as a basic component — contemporary physicists think that much smaller parts might be basic). Philosophical atomism is associated with DEMOCRITUS, EPICURUS, LUCRETIUS, and many more modern philosophers of nature. (*See also* LOGICAL ATOMISM)

attribute *See* QUALITY / ATTRIBUTE / PROPERTY.

attributes, divine *See* DIVINE ATTRIBUTES.

Augustine, St. (354-430) Philosopher and theologian, born in N. Africa; converted to Christianity in 386. An important figure in the establishment of Christianity as an intellectual and political force, and in the transition from ancient to medieval thought; the first important

Christian philosopher. ['aw-GUS-tin', or sometimes 'AW-gus-teen']

Austin, John (1790-1859) English legal philosopher known for his position that LAW 1 is the command of the sovereign.

Austin, J(ohn) L(angshaw) (1911-1960) English (Oxford) philosopher; a leading figure in ORDINARY LANGUAGE PHILOSOPHY. He drew philosophical conclusions from ANALYSES of our uses of language in general, and of particular philosophically relevant words.

authoritarian A government, church, etc., that demands strict and unquestioning obedience, and thus denies freedom of thought or action, is authoritarian.

authenticity — *See* BAD FAITH / GOOD FAITH / AUTHENTICITY / INAUTHENTICITY.

automata These are (arguably) mindless devices that imitate the intelligent and goal-directed actions of people — robots, for example. DESCARTES thought that animals were automata — merely physical "mechanisms," without mind. ['automata' is plural; singular 'automaton'; 'aw-TOM-a-ta', 'aw-TOM-a-ton'] *See also* ARTIFICIAL INTELLIGENCE, CYBERNETICS.

autonomy / heteronomy Autonomy is self-governance — the ability or right to determine one's own actions and beliefs. Some ethical theories see the respect for autonomy as a central ethical principle. Heteronomy is its opposite: dependence on others. *See also* PATERNALISM.

Averroës (also spelled 'Averrhoës'; in Arabic, ibn-Rushd) (1126-1198) Spanish-born Arab philosopher; important

Islamic philosopher, influenced by ARISTOTLE and PLATO. ['uh-VER-oh-eez' or 'a-ver-OH-eez']

Avicenna (Arabic full name Ab-u 'Al-i al-Husayn ibn 'Abd-All-ah ibn S-in-a) (980-1037) Persian philosopher, the most influential medieval Islam philosopher. His comprehensive philosophical system was based largely on ARISTOTLE, and was a strong influence on THOMAS AQUINAS.

axiology The study of the general theory of values.

axiomatic theory *See* AXIOM / POSTULATE.

axiom / postulate An axiom is a statement regarded as obviously true, used as a starting point for deriving other statements. An axiomatic THEORY is one that is based on axioms. Not every theory is axiomatic: some don't have such basic statements. 'Postulate' is often used to mean the same thing, though sometimes it refers only to such statements within a particular theory, while axioms are basic and obvious statements common to many theories (for example, the basic laws of LOGIC). 'Postulation' refers to the act of ASSUMPTION, often of the existence of something, for theoretical purposes. (*See also* POSIT.)

Ayer, (Sir) A(lfred) J(ules) (1910-1989) English philosopher; his book *Language, Truth and Logic* presented LOGICAL POSITIVISM in a vigorous and influential way. ['AY-er']

B

Bacon, Francis (Baron Verulam and Viscount St. Albans) (1561-1626) English philosopher and scientist. Best known for his work on scientific method, he is often considered the father of modern science.

Bacon, Roger (1214?-?1292) English philosopher and scientist, known as 'Doctor Mirabilis'. An influential early EPISTEMOLOGIST and theorist of scientific method.

bad faith / good faith / authenticity / inauthenticity
These are all terms associated with SARTRE'S EXISTENTIALISM. Bad faith is one's attempt to deny one's own FREEDOM (to try to avoid existential ANGUISH – the anxiety Sartre thought the recognition of one's freedom brings) by trying to pretend that one's actions, values, or preferences are determined by something in one's past – heredity, environment, social expectations, objective values, personality, etc. Good faith, its opposite, is the accepting that one is the author of, and responsible for, actions, values, and preferences. Authenticity is a state thought praiseworthy by existentialists; it is a state of good faith, in which one actively creates one's long- and short-term ideals, projects, and plans, and owns up to having them and to having created them.

"ball of wax" example
DESCARTES used this example to show the necessity of believing in physical SUBSTANCE. Imagine you see a ball of wax, at room temperature. Put it next to the fire, and in a while, all its characteristics have changed: its shape, colour, odour, hardness, etc.

Yet it is the same object we saw earlier (not something else). Thus sameness in this sense cannot be explained in terms of having the same characteristics; so there must be something other than characteristics — an unchanging and invisible substance — which accounts for this sameness. *See also* IDENTITY 3, PROBLEM OF IDENTITY, QUALITY / ATTRIBUTE / PROPERTY.

Barthes, Roland (1915-1980) French philosopher associated with the STRUCTURALISTS, known for his application of that theory to literary criticism.

basic action If someone did x by doing y, then x is not a basic ACTION (it's a non-basic action). Sally murdered Sam by shooting him, so Sally's murdering Sam is not a basic action. Sally shot Sam by discharging her revolver, so Sally's shooting Sam isn't a basic action either. What action of Sally's was basic? Perhaps her moving her finger (when she shot the revolver) — she didn't do this by doing something else. This distinction has relevance in ACTION THEORY.

basic statement The truth or falsity of some statements is determined by appeal to some others (by means of LOGIC or scientific method), but some philosophers think that there must be a starting point: basic statements. Whether there are basic statements, what they are, and why they are acceptable, are all controversial questions. *See also* AXIOM / POSTULATE, LOGICAL ATOMISM, PROTOCOL SENTENCES.

Bayesian An adjective referring to a variety of related aspects of PROBABILITY theory, associated with the work of Arthur Bayes, English mathematician. **1.** Bayes' theorem is a mathematical formula relating conditional and prior probability. **2.** 'Bayesianism' sometimes refers to the view that probability should be understood as subjective; or 3. to the view that rational choice is choice that maximizes EXPECTED UTILITY. [Pronounced 'bayz', 'BAYZ-ian']

Bayle, Pierre (1607-1706) French ENLIGHTENMENT philosopher, an important influence on HUME, VOLTAIRE, and others because of his destructive SCEPTICAL attacks on prior views.

Beauvoir, Simone de (1908-1986) French writer and philosopher, known for her EXISTENTIALISM and her FEMINISM.

becoming / being Being is whatever exists. Some philosophers thought that in the real realm of being, nothing changes; thus the realm of becoming, the visible world where things change, was thought to be unreal or "less real." Philosophers who hold this view face the necessity of explaining how we know about the real world, and what the visible world has to do with it. These worries were a central feature of ancient Greek philosophy, and often also concerns of MODERN PHILOSOPHY and science.

beetle in the box WITTGENSTEIN tells the following philosophical fable:

Suppose each person had something he/she calls a 'beetle' in a box, but could see only what's in his/her box. It's possible that each person has something different, or even nothing at all, in his/her box, or that the contents of some person's box are constantly changing. The word 'beetle' would then have no use in our language.

This fable can be taken to be an attack on the idea that there are PRIVATE objects—for example, mental events that only the person having them can know about. At least on the idea that we can talk about such private things in public language (*see* PRIVATE LANGUAGE ARGUMENT).

begging the question *See* CIRCULAR REASONING / DEFINITION.

behaviourism Early in the twentieth century, many psychologists decided that INTROSPECTION was not a good basis for the science of the mind; instead they decided to concentrate only on external, observable behaviour (*see* PRIVACY). Methodological (psychological) behaviourism is the view that only external behaviour should be investigated by science. METAPHYSICAL or ANALYTICAL behaviourism is the philosophical view that public behaviour is all there is—that this is what we're talking about when we refer to mental events or characteristics in others, and even in ourselves. It's a form of MATERIALISM. J. B. Watson and B. F. Skinner (*See* SCIENTISTS) were two American psychologists who were very influential in arguing for methodological and analytical behaviourism. [The American spelling of these words omits the 'u']

being *See* BECOMING / BEING.

being for itself / in itself *See* IN ITSELF / FOR ITSELF.

belief *See* KNOWLEDGE / BELIEF.

benevolence Good-willing; in moral theory, it often refers to a SYMPATHETIC feeling toward other people. HUME thought that benevolence was the basis of ethics.

Bentham, Jeremy (1748-1832) English founder of UTILITARIANISM, influential in moral and political theory.

Bergson, Henri (Louis) (1859-1941) French philosopher in whose work EVOLUTION plays a central role. Among his central notions is the "ÉLAN VITAL" — the non-MATERIALISTIC vital force supposed to cause change and development. He was a champion of INTUITION against rationalistic "conceptual" thought.

Berkeley, George (1685-1753) Irish philosopher, Bishop of Cloyne; known for his EMPIRICIST and IDEALIST METAPHYSICS and EPISTEMOLOGY. Berkeley rejected the idea that a world independent of PERCEPTIONS can be inferred from them; perceptions are all there is. (But they can exist externally and independently of us — in the mind of God.) Since only individual particular perceptions are possible, he argued against the possibility of ABSTRACT ideas. His views may be construed as a form of PHENOMENALISM. ['BARK-lee': 'BERK-lee' is the pronunciation of the name of the California city named after the philosopher.]

best of all possible worlds A phrase associated with LEIBNIZ, who believed that God, being perfectly good, knowing, and powerful, could not have created anything less than perfect; thus this world (despite how it sometimes appears, especially on Monday morning) is the best of all possible worlds (*see* PROBLEM OF EVIL).

biconditional A material biconditional (sometimes merely called a 'biconditional') is a TRUTH-FUNCTIONAL connective. It is true when both sentences it connects are true, or when both are false; it is false when the sentences have different TRUTH-VALUES. It is symbolized by the triple-bar (≡) or the double-arrow (↔) (*see* SYM-BOLS OF SENTENTIAL LOGIC), and may be interpreted as "if and only if" (sometimes abbreviated 'iff'). It is called the biconditional because it means the same as a conjunction of two CONDITIONALS: p ≡ q is equivalent to (p ⊃ q) & (q ⊃ p). A logical biconditional is a biconditional that is LOGICALLY TRUE. Another name for the material biconditional is 'material equivalence'.

bioethics The ethics involved in various sorts of biology-related activities, mostly centring on medical matters. Examples of issues considered in bioethics are abortion, mind control (e.g., through drugs), genetic control, euthanasia, and *in vitro* fertilization.

binary predicate *See* PREDICATE.

binary relation *See* RELATIONS.

bivalence —*see* law of the excluded middle, in LAWS OF THOUGHT.

Black, Max (1909-1988) Russian-born American philosopher, professor at Cornell University. Influential in the philosophies of LOGIC, mathematics, language, science, and knowledge.

bodily interchange This is what would happen if the same person existed at one time in one body and at another time in another body, for example, through REINCARNATION, or in a variety of science-fiction ways, (such as brain or memory transplant). The topic is important to think about not only in religious contexts or as entertainment, but as a THOUGHT-EXPERIMENT about PERSONAL IDENTITY.

Boethius, (Anicius Manlius Severinus) (c. 480-524) Roman philosopher and statesman, translator of Aristotle. Best known for his influential work in LOGIC, and for his book *The Consolation of Philosophy*. ['bo-EE-thee-us']

Bolzano, Bernard (1781-1848) Czech philosopher, theologian, logician, and mathematician. His work in EPISTEMOLOGY and LOGIC, unrecognized in his time, has received recent attention.

Bonaventure (in Italian, Bonaventura), St. (Original name, Giovanni di Fidanza) (1221-1274) Italian SCHOLASTIC philosopher / theologian. His work is strongly influenced by St. AUGUSTINE.

Bonhoeffer, Dietrich (1906-1945) German theologian. Active in the resistance to Hitler, he died in a Nazi concentration camp. His radically secularized and ecumenical religious views have been of great interest in contemporary THEOLOGY.

Boole, George (1815-1864) English mathematician responsible for the development of the idea of treating variables in logic (*see* SYMBOLS OF QUANTIFIER LOGIC) in ways analogous to those in algebra; this was the first real step in the development of modern logic.

bound variable *See* SYMBOLS OF QUANTIFIER LOGIC.

Boyle, Robert *See* SCIENTISTS.

bracketing HUSSERL's term, referring to the process of suspending normal ASSUMPTIONS 1 and PRESUPPOSITIONS. He thought that by "bracketing off" the assumptions of science we could see things as they fundamentally appear to CONSCIOUSNESS. *See also* PHENOMENOLOGY.

Bradley, F(rancis) H(erbert) (1846-1924) English IDEALIST philosopher, known for his works on LOGIC, METAPHYSICS, and ethics. Outside the British EMPIRICIST tradition, his work is more in the continental HEGELian spirit. His central metaphysical notion is "the ABSOLUTE" – a coherent and comprehensive whole that harmonizes the diversity and SELF-CONTRADICTIONS of appearances.

brain in a vat Imagine that you are, and always have been, merely a brain suspended in a vat of nutritive liquid, connected to a computer that feeds you electronic signals (thereby simulating sense experience). All your experiences are thus hallucinations (*see* ILLUSION / HALLUCINATION / DELUSION). Have you any good reason to think you are not a brain in a vat? This thought experiment, suggested by Hilary PUTNAM, is used by philosophers to consider the form of SCEPTICISM about the external world it raises.

Brentano, Franz (1838-1917) German philosopher and psychologist, an important influence on later CONTINENTAL philosophers; known for his theory of "INTENTIONALITY" 2; the view that mental acts refer to (sometimes "inexistent") things beyond themselves.

Bridgman, Percy – *See* SCIENTISTS.

Broad, C(harlie) D(unbar) (1887-1971) English philosopher who contributed to a wide variety of topics; a collector and systematizer of traditional philosophical ideas who nevertheless took account of contemporary philosophy and science.

Brouwer, Luitzen Egbertus Jan (1881-1966) Dutch mathematician, the founder of mathematical INTUITIONISM, with important work in the philosophy of mathematics.

Bruno, Giordano (1548-1600) Italian Renaissance philosopher. He worked in various European countries after religious persecution forced him to flee Italy; burned as a heretic. His work is now seen as an important step toward the scientific views of nature that followed.

Buber, Martin (1878-1965) Austrian Jewish philosopher and theologian, worked in Germany and Palestine. Best known for his thought on the differences between the relationships we have with things and with people: he called the latter the "I-thou" relationship.

bundle theory HUME's theory of PERSONAL IDENTITY. He argued that since we can't perceive any continuing self in us, our idea of a person, which has to come from PERCEPTION to be valid, can't be of a continuing mental SUBSTANCE. All we can perceive in ourselves is a continuously changing "bundle" of mental events, so this is what our CONCEPT of the self must consist of.

burden of proof When there is a disagreement, it's sometimes the case that one side is expected to prove its case, and if it can't, the other wins by default. The side that must provide proof is said to have the burden of proof. If one position is surprising, or unorthodox, or if it runs counter to other well-accepted beliefs, then that position tends to have the burden of proof. Thus, for example, people who claim that we have been regularly visited by aliens from outer space have the burden of proof.

Buridan, Jean (1295-1356) French philosopher and scientist; work on physics, LOGIC, and METAPHYSICS. His thought on will and reason resulted in his association with the example now known as BURIDAN'S ASS.

Buridan's ass BURIDAN believed that one must do what and only what seems to one to be the greatest good. One problem raised by this position is illustrated by the story known as Buridan's ass (though Buridan himself is not responsible for this story): imagine a hungry ass standing between two equal and equidistant piles of hay. Neither would seem more desirable to it than the other, so if Buridan's principle were right, the animal would starve to death.

Burke, Edmund (1729-1797) British statesman and political thinker, associated with conservative political views.

Butler, Bishop Joseph. (1692-1752) English theologian and moralist, known for his work on moral psychology and THEOLOGY.

C

calculus An abstract system of symbols, aimed at calculating something. A calculus is interpreted when its symbols are given meaning by relating them to things in the real world. Some philosophers think of the various sciences as interpreted calculi. One can call each symbol-system of SYMBOLIC LOGIC a 'calculus': for example, the SENTENTIAL and QUANTIFIER calculi. ('Calculus' is singular; plural: 'calculi')

calculus, felicity / felicific / pleasure-pain / hedonic / happiness. *See* FELICIFIC CALCULUS.

Calvin, John (original name Jean Chauvin or Caulvin) (1509-1564) French (lived in Switzerland) theologian and religious reformer. His moral, theological, and social views ("Calvinism") have been extremely influential.

Camus, Albert (1913-1960) Algerian-born French novelist and philosopher, associated with the EXISTENTIALISTS.

canon A basic and important rule.

Cantor, Georg (1845-1918) Russian-born German mathematician and logician, best known for his creation of SET theory.

Carnap, Rudolf (1891-1970) German-born philosopher who spent his later life in the U.S., to which he transplanted LOGICAL POSITIVISM when the VIENNA CIRCLE disbanded in pre-World War II Austria. He is important also for his work on philosophy of science and LOGIC.

Cartesian This means 'pertaining to DESCARTES'. Cartesianism is a school of thought derived from Descartes' philosophy.

Cartesian doubt A philosophical method (associated with DESCARTES) in which one begins by assuming that any belief which could be doubted is false — even the most ordinary ASSUMPTIONS[1] of common sense. One then searches for a starting point that is INDUBITABLE.

Cassirer, Ernst (1874-1945) German philosopher (working in his later life in the U.S.) who extended KANT's views in considering symbolic representation and culture.

casuistry The determination of right and wrong by reasoning involving general principles applied to particular cases, taking into account their particular characteristics. Because casuists (especially in religious contexts) sometimes reasoned in overly complex ways to silly conclusions, this word has come to have disparaging overtones. ['KAZH-you-is-tree']

categorial logic The theory of the logical relations between sentences with the following forms: All A's are B's; No A's are B's; Some A's are B's; Some A's are not B's. These are the standard forms of the categorial propositions. See also A / E / I / O PROPOSITIONS.

categorical / hypothetical imperative KANT's distinction. An imperative is a command. 'Categorical' means absolute — not dependent on particular aims or circumstances; 'hypothetical' means relative to, depending on, particular aims or circumstances. Thus, 'Tell the truth' is a categorical imperative, but 'If it is to everyone's benefit, tell the truth' and 'If you want others to trust you, tell the truth' are hypothetical imperatives. Kant argued that hypothetical imperatives, while sometimes giving useful practical advice, do not express the truths of morality, which are expressed only by categorical imperatives. He argued further that there is one command central to all morality—*the* categorical imperative: Act in a way such that the general rule behind your action could consistently be willed to be a universal law. He argued that this was equivalent to saying that others should be treated as ends, never as means only.

categories Used by ARISTOTLE and KANT to refer to our most basic concepts. Kant thought these were A PRIORI, and they included CAUSATION and SUBSTANCE.

category mistake Gilbert RYLE gave this example of a category mistake: someone is shown a number of classroom and administrative buildings, libraries, student residences, etc., but says, "I have seen all those, but where is the university?" His mistake was to think that the university is just another building, whereas the university is in a different category. Ryle argued that some philosophical mistakes—for instance, the separation of mind from body and its behaviour—are thus made by people who don't understand what categories their concepts belong in.

catharsis ARISTOTLE's term for the purging or cleansing of the emotions that he thought happened to the audience at the end of a dramatic tragedy, when pity and terror produced in the audience are calmed. [also spelled 'katharsis']

causal chain A series of events in which each event causes the next.

causal explanation *See* EXPLANATION.

causa sui *See* CAUSE-OF-ITSELF.

causation The relation that holds between a CAUSE and its effect. Also called 'causality'.

cause That which brings something about, or, in a wider and old-fashioned sense, merely EXPLAINS it. (For this wider sense, *see* EFFICIENT / FORMAL / MATERIAL / FINAL CAUSES.) Long-standing philosophical problems are concerned with the nature of cause, and how we find out about it. HUME argued that we think that A causes B when A's have regularly been followed by B's in the past (i.e., have been "constantly conjoined" with B's); but that the notion that A has a "power" to produce B "necessarily" (*see* NECESSARY / CONTINGENT TRUTH) is not something we can observe, so this is not a legitimate part of the notion of cause. Critics object that this fails to distinguish between causal connections and mere accidental but universal regularities. [The adjectival form of this word is 'causal'—be careful not to spell this 'casual'.]

cause, false *See* FALSE CAUSE.

cause-of-itself (Latin; *causa sui*) Narrowly, a thing that causes itself to exist (or to be the way it is). God is commonly thought to be the only thing that is capable of this. This notion is difficult to understand, given that, in the common notion of CAUSE, for x to cause y, x must exist before y does, and it's nonsense to think of something existing before it itself does. A broader (and more old-fashioned) notion thinks of cause as EXPLANATION. This does not lead to the same absurdity, but has its own problems: how can something provide the explanation for its own existence?

cause, proximate / remote *See* PROXIMATE / REMOTE CAUSE.

causes, efficient / formal / material / final *See* EFFICIENT / FORMAL / MATERIAL / FINAL CAUSES.

causes / reasons *See* REASONS / CAUSES.

cave In *The Republic*, PLATO imagines a group of prisoners chained inside a cave, who never see anything in the outside world; all they see are shadows cast on the wall of the cave by objects inside the cave that are copies of real things outside. This is presented as an analogy to how Plato sees our status: what we experience is not reality, but merely a shadowy representation of it. The philosopher's job is to figure out what reality might be like. (See also PLATONIC FORMS).

central-state materialism *See* MATERIALISM.

certain A belief is called 'certain' in ordinary talk when it is believed very strongly, or when one is unable to think, or even imagine, that it might be false. Philosophers often don't want to rely on such subjective and psychological matters, and demand proof that some belief really is beyond rational doubt.

ceteris paribus (Latin: "other things being equal") This is used in comparing two things, assuming they differ only in the one characteristic under consideration. For example, it could be said that, ceteris paribus, a simple theory is better than a complicated one; though if everything else is not equal—if, for example, the simpler theory has fewer true predictions – then it might not be better. ['KEH' or 'SEH' + '-ter-iss PAR-uh-bus']

chain, causal *See* CAUSAL CHAIN.

chance Something happens by chance when it is not fully DETERMINED by previous events – when previous events do not necessarily bring it about, or make it the way it is; in other words, when it's a random event. Sometimes, however, we speak of chance events as those we're unable to predict with certainty, though they might be determined in unknown ways. (For example, how a flipped coin turns up may be fully determined by how it's flipped, but in practice, we don't and can't do the measurements and calculations, so we say it's a matter of chance.) We can sometimes know the PROBABILITY of chance events in advance.

chaos 1. Early philosophers used this term to refer to the unformed and disorderly state of things which, they supposed, preceded the imposition of order that produced the universe (the COSMOS). **2.** The term has been used recently (in 'chaos theory') to refer to a branch of mathematical study concerned with complex and in some ways unpredictable phenomena such as the weather.

chimera In Greek mythology, this is a monster with a lion's head, goat's body, and snake's tail. By extension, in philosophy this means a non-existent object which we imagine by combining features of real things. ['ky-MEER-a' or 'kuh-MEER-a']

Chomsky, (Avram) Noam (b. 1928) American linguist (known for ground-breaking work in SEMANTIC theory) and philosopher (associated with the INNATENESS hypothesis.) Recently in the public eye for his strong left-wing political views.

Cicero (Marcus Tullius) (106-43 B.C.) Roman orator and statesman, writer of works on politics and oratory.

circle, vicious *See* VICIOUS CIRCLE.

Circle, Vienna *See* VIENNA CIRCLE.

circular reasoning / definition A DEFINITION is circular (and thus useless) when the term to be defined, or a version of it, occurs in the definition; for example, the definition of 'free action' as 'action that is freely done'. Circular reasoning defends some statement by assuming the truth of that statement; e.g.:

"Why do you think what the Bible says is true?"

"Because the Bible is the Word of God."

"How do you know that it is the Word of God?"

"Because it says so in the Bible, and everything there is true."

Reasoning that is bad because circular is said to be a 'vicious circle'. Some philosophers argue that not all circles are vicious—some sorts of circular reasoning are acceptable, for example, when the circle is wide enough. Circular reasoning is also known as 'begging the question'. Careless speakers sometimes think that this is synonymous with 'raising the question'; it isn't. Begging the question is sometimes called by its Latin name, *'petitio principii'* ['peh-TIT-ee-oh prin-KIP-ee-ee' or 'pi-TISH-ee-oh prin-SIP-ee-ee'] "postulation of the beginning."

civil rights *See* RIGHTS.

clairvoyance *See* PARANORMAL PHENOMENA.

class *See* SET.

clear and distinct ideas DESCARTES (and others) have used this to refer to the kind of ideas they thought philosophers should seek as the foundation for any other beliefs, and which are completely reliable or CERTAIN. An idea is clear according to Descartes, when it is "present and apparent to an attentive mind"; and distinct when it is "so precise and different from other objects that it contains within itself nothing but what is clear." There is some problem in interpreting just what Descartes meant here, and in showing why this sort of idea might be especially or completely reliable.

coercion *See* COMPULSION.

coextensive Two TERMS or PREDICATES are coextensive when they in fact apply to exactly the same objects (*see* EXTENSION / INTENSION).

cogito ergo sum (Latin: "I think, therefore I exist") DESCARTES' famous argument (sometimes called 'the cogito', for short), which he took to be the starting point in his search for CERTAINTY. Whatever else he might be mistaken about, he reasoned, he could not be mistaken that he was thinking, because even mistaken thinking is thinking. It followed that he must exist—at least as a thinking thing. ['KO-' or 'KAH' + '-gee-to air-go soom']

cognition The mental process by which we get KNOWLEDGE.

cognitivism / noncognitivism Cognitivism is the position that something can be known. Ethical cognitivism is the view that ethical statements are statements about (supposed) facts and thus are true or false, and might be known to be true or false. This is opposed to the noncognitivist position that ethical statements are not knowable. A species of ethical noncognitivism is EMOTIVISM, which argues that ethical statements are not fact-stating, but are expressions of approval or disapproval (like 'Hooray for that!'), or invitations to action (like 'Please do that!') and are thus neither true nor false, and not knowable.

coherence / incoherence A SET of beliefs or sentences is coherent when it fits together in a logical way—that is, when everything in the set is consistent, or when the items in it CONFIRM others in it. A set in which one item would be false, or probably false, given the truth of others is not coherent (is incoherent). A coherentist position is one that claims that the coherence of a group of beliefs or sentences is what counts for their truth or reliability—and perhaps the only thing that counts.

coherence theory of truth *See* TRUTH.

collectively / distributively What applies to a group collectively applies to it as a whole only, i.e., not to its individual members (not distributively). The atoms that constitute a pig collectively, but not distributively, outweigh a fly.

commitment A binding OBLIGATION voluntarily undertaken by the person thus obligated. EXISTENTIALISTS hold that one freely and arbitrarily makes up one's commitments, and that this is the only source of one's moral obligation.

common consent argument for God's existence The supposed fact that so many cultures in all historical periods have believed in God is given as evidence of His existence. Common criticisms of this argument are that not all cultures share belief in God, and that it wouldn't prove anything even if they did. Here's a particularly bad version of this argument:

The Bible has been translated into hundreds of different languages, but in every single translation, it says that God exists! So He must exist.

common-sense realism *See* NAIVE REALISM.

communism *See* SOCIALISM / COMMUNISM.

commutativity *See* SYMMETRIC / ASYMMETRIC / NON-SYMMETRIC.

compatiblism Any philosophical position that claims that two things are compatible (they can both exist at once). In particular, this word is often used to refer to the view that FREE WILL and DETERMINISM are compatible — that is, that people's ACTIONS are (sometimes) free even though they are fully causally determined. They argue that we're not free when we're acting under COMPULSION (that is, *forced* to act), but that this is a different thing from the action's being determined or caused.

complement The complement of one SET is another set containing everything not in the first. The complement of the set of pigs includes all non-pigs (cows, planets, toes, days of the week, etc.). If 'p' stands for the set of pigs, then '-p' stands for its complement. The complement of the term 'pigs' is the term 'non-pigs'.

completeness / incompleteness These terms have a variety of technical senses, but in a common use, a LOGICAL system is complete when every LOGICALLY TRUE sentence is DERIVABLE, and otherwise incomplete.

complex ideas *See* SIMPLE / COMPLEX IDEAS.

composition The fallacy of composition is the incorrect reasoning from properties of parts of a whole to properties of the whole itself. For instance, it's true that each atom of a pig weighs less than one gram, but it's a mistake to conclude that since the pig is composed of nothing but these atoms, that the pig weighs less than one gram.

compulsion An ACTION is said to be done under compulsion (also known as 'constraint' or 'coercion') when it is "forced" by internal or external circumstances, and thus the doer of that action can't be held morally RESPONSIBLE for doing it. If you steal something, for example, because someone is forcing you to do it at gunpoint, or because you are a kleptomaniac (i.e., you have the psychological disorder that is supposed to create an irresistible tendency to steal), that doesn't make your action any better, but it does mean that you're not to blame. COMPATIBLISTS about FREE WILL argue that compulsion is the sort of cause that makes one unfree and not responsible, but when one's action is caused (DETERMINED) but not due to compulsion, one is free and responsible.

Comte, (Isadore) Auguste (Marie François) (1798-1857) French POSITIVIST philosopher. He emphasized the evolution of thought toward scientific, EMPIRICAL explanation. He is credited with founding the science of sociology.

concept 1. In ordinary talk, this word often has little meaning, and is best omitted when it's just a pretentious synonym for 'idea'. **2.** Philosophers may use this word to refer to the ability to categorize things; thus to say that someone has the concept of *duck* is to say that that person can sort things correctly into ducks and non-ducks. A concept is sometimes distinguished from a percept, which is a particular mental item had while sensing a particular thing. A concept, then, may be thought to be a generalization or ABSTRACTION from one or many percepts. Thus a percept is sometimes called a particular idea, and a concept a general or abstract idea.

conceptual truth A statement that is true merely because of the nature of the CONCEPTS that make it up. The fact that all bachelors are unmarried is a conceptual truth, because the concept of being a bachelor involves being unmarried. Compare the fact that snow is white: this is not a conceptual truth, because being white, despite being true of snow, is not part of the concept of snow. We can imagine, consistent with our concept of snow, that snow is always green. (Substitute 'word' for 'concept' in this definition, and it turns into the definition of 'ANALYTIC TRUTH'.)

conclusion *See* ARGUMENT.

concrete Contrasted with 'ABSTRACT', something is concrete when it is particular and real (perhaps material — *see* MATERIALISM). The FALLACY of misplaced concreteness mistakenly argues that something abstract is real (*see* REIFICATION).

Condillac, Étienne Bonnot de (1715-1780) French philosopher, with influential works on theory of knowledge. ['kon-dee-yak']

conditional A statement of the form 'if p then q', for example, 'If it's raining, then you'll get wet'. What this sort of statement means (and what would make it true) is a surprisingly complicated matter, but a core of that meaning is MODELLED by the (much simpler) material conditional in SENTENTIAL LOGIC. A material conditional of the form 'if p then q' is defined as a statement that is true when p is false or q is true (or both); so it is false only when p is true and q is false. The first sentence in this material conditional is called the 'antecedent', the second the 'consequent'. To symbolize this sentence we connect letters representing the antecedent and consequent by the horseshoe (⊃) or the arrow (→) (*see* SYMBOLS OF SENTENTIAL LOGIC). To *see* why the material conditional is only a rough match for the English conditional, consider the English sentence 'If Bolivia is in Asia, then pigs fly.' Is this true or false or neither? It's hard to say. But suppose we translate this into symbolic logic as 'B ⊃ P'. Now the antecedent of this material conditional 'B' ('Bolivia is in Asia') is false, so 'B ⊃ P' is true. This and other strange results of modelling the English conditional by the material conditional are known as the PARADOXES of the material conditional. It's clear also that the material conditional does not model the COUNTERFACTUAL. A material conditional is also known as a material implication, though 'implication' can also refer to a relation between whole statements. Material conditionals should be distinguished from strict implications: these are conditionals that are LOGICALLY TRUE, for example, 'If some pigs are sloppy eaters, then some sloppy eaters are pigs.'

conditional, contrary-to-fact *See* COUNTERFACTUAL.

conditional probability *See* PROBABILITY.

condition, necessary / sufficient *See* NECESSARY / SUFFICIENT CONDITION.

confirmation/disconfirmation/verification/falsification Confirmation is the collection of evidence to show that a statement is true. Because there might be some evidence even for a false statement, a statement might be confirmed though false. Collecting evidence that a statement is false is called 'disconfirmation'. 'Verification' means 'confirmation', and 'falsification' means 'disconfirmation', though one tends to speak of a statement as having been verified (or falsified) only if the statement is really true (or false), and has been shown to be so by the evidence.

Condorcet, Marquis de (1743-1797) French mathematician, philosopher, and social theorist. ['kon-dor-say']

Condorcet paradox *See* VOTER'S PARADOX **2.**

conjunction The logical relation expressed in English by connecting two sentences by 'and'; also the sentence thus formed. The sentences connected in a conjunction are called 'conjuncts'. A conjunction is true when both conjuncts are true, and false otherwise. Thus the sentence 'It's raining and it's Tuesday' is true when both 'It's raining' and 'It's Tuesday' are true. If one or both conjuncts are false, the conjunction is false. A conjunction is symbolized in logic by connecting letters standing for the conjuncts with an ampersand (&) or a dot (.) (*see* SYMBOLS OF SENTENTIAL LOGIC)

connotation *See* DENOTATION / CONNOTATION.

conscience This is the sense of right and wrong. It is sometimes supposed that this is a way we have of knowing moral truths, perhaps by some sort of reliable internal "voice" or sense-perception, perhaps provided by God, which tells us moral facts. [Students sometimes confuse this word with 'CONSCIOUS'].

consciousness 1. The state that we are in when awake: mental events are going on. **2.** Awareness of something. (You aren't usually conscious of the position of your tongue). **3.** = mind (though it might be that the mind exists even while we are asleep or not aware of anything). The fact that we are conscious is supposed by some to distinguish people from machines and other non-living things, and perhaps from (at least the lower) animals. *See also* SELF-CONSCIOUSNESS.

consequent *See* CONDITIONAL.

consequentialism The position that people's actions are right or wrong because of their consequences (their results). This sort of ethical theory is also called 'TELEOLOGICAL', and is contrasted with deontological theories (associated with KANT and others), which hold that results of actions are morally irrelevant. Thus, for example, a Kantian might think that lying is always wrong just in itself, whereas a consequentialist might think that lying is morally permissible in those circumstances in which the lie results in good consequences overall.

consistency A SET of statements is consistent if it is logically possible that all the statements in that set are true. It is inconsistent if one statement CONTRADICTS another, or if a contradiction results from reasoning from the set. For example, these three statements form an inconsistent set:

Fred is good at logic.

Nobody who failed this test is good at logic.

Fred failed this test.

Note that there can be a consistent set in which some, or all, the statements are false. The two false statements, 'Pigs fly' and 'Grass is always purple' make a consistent set: they don't contradict each other, and no contradiction arises from assuming both of them. Each is false, but each might have been true, and both could have been true together. The set consisting of this one statement 'It's raining and it's not raining' is inconsistent, because this statement is SELF-CONTRADICTORY.

constant *See* SYMBOLS OF QUANTIFIER LOGIC.

constant conjunction *See* CAUSE.

constative *See* PERFORMATIVE / CONSTATIVE.

constitutive / regulative rule A regulative rule merely tells people what to do or not to do (e.g., 'Keep off the grass'). Constitutive rules (according to SEARLE) may "create or define new forms of behaviour" and "often have the form: X counts as Y." Thus, the rule 'Moving the ball across the goal line while in play counts as a touchdown' creates a new form of behaviour (a touchdown, non-existent without this rule). ['con-STIT-you-tiv']

constraint *See* COMPULSION.

constructive dilemma An argument with this form:
> Either A or B.
> If A then C; if B then D.
> Therefore C or D.

Another, simpler form of constructive dilemma is:
> Either A or B.
> If A then C; if B then C.
> Therefore C.

(*See also* DILEMMA).

constructive existence proof In mathematics, one gives a constructive existence proof of some mathematical entity when one produces an example of it, or at least gives a method for producing an example. INTUITIONISTS in mathematics may, for example, reject the existence of infinity because no constructive existence proof of it can be given.

construct, theoretical *See* theoretical ENTITIES / CONSTRUCTS.

contemplation Meditation, thoughtfulness. Some philosophers think that the contemplative life — one filled with thought (especially philosophical thought!) — is the best or happiest. It's not obvious that this is true.

context The relevant surroundings of something. In LOGIC, the context of a group of words is the rest of the words in its sentence. One logically interesting distinction between contexts is their OPAQUE / TRANSPARENT character. In ethics, context is relevant to those who think that the surroundings of some act are relevant to its rightness or wrongness.

contiguity Proximity (touching) in space or time ('spatial' or 'TEMPORAL contiguity'). Two events are spatially and temporally contiguous when there is neither space between them nor time between their occurrence.

continental philosophy A major tradition in philosophy, associated with nineteenth- and twentieth- century philosophers on the (European) continent (though done elsewhere too); central figures are HEGEL, HUSSERL, HEIDEGGER, SARTRE, FOUCAULT, and HABERMAS. The contrast implied is with ANALYTIC philosophy; though nowadays it's hard to provide any generalizations about the thought of either large and diverse group, and these terms tend to be derogatory epithets used to name one's competition. Continental philosophers are sometimes thought to be more friendly than analytic philosophers to RATIONALISM and to SPECULATIVE philosophy.

Contingency To say that a true (or false) statement is contingent is to deny that it *must* be true (or false). METAPHYSICAL contingency is contrasted with necessary truth and falsity (*see* NECESSARY / CONTINGENT TRUTH); logical contingency is contrasted with LOGICAL TRUTH AND FALSITY. Each sort is sometimes simply called 'contingency'. This makes things confusing.

contingents, problem of future *See* PROBLEM OF FUTURE CONTINGENTS.

continuum 1. A process of gradual development with no sudden changes. **2.** A series with no gaps in it, i.e., continuous, not composed of discrete elements. Time is a continuum if between any two times, no matter how close, there is a third. ['con-TIN-you-um']

contra-causal freedom LIBERTARIANS sometimes believe that a free ACTION — one we're RESPONSIBLE for — could only be one that is not caused by previous events. Thus, the sort of freedom they attribute to some of our actions is contra-causal (*see* FREE WILL).

contractarianism *See* SOCIAL CONTRACT.

contradiction / contrary Two statements are contradictory when the truth of one logically requires the falsity of the other, and the falsity of one requires the truth of the other — in other words, when it is impossible that both are true, and it is impossible that both are false. 'It's raining' and 'It's not raining' are contradictory: exactly one of them must be true. Two statements are contraries when it is impossible that they are both true, though they might both be false. 'No pigs fly' and 'All pigs fly' are contraries, not contradictories. It is logically impossible that both of them are true, though they both might be false (were it the case that some, but not all, pigs fly). One can also call a SELF-CONTRADICTION a 'contradiction'.

contradiction, law of *See* LAW OF CONTRADICTION.

contraposition 1. A rule of SENTENTIAL LOGIC that says that from any sentence of the form 'If p then q' one may reason correctly to the corresponding sentence of the form 'If not q then not p'. **2.** A rule of CATEGORIAL LOGIC that says that one may create a logically equivalent sentence from any categorial sentence by replacing its subject terms with the COMPLEMENT of its PREDICATE term, and by replacing its predicate term with the complement of its subject term. For example, the contrapositive of 'All bats are mammals' is 'All non-mammals are non-bats'.

contrary *See* CONTRADICTION / CONTRARY.

contrary-to-fact conditional *See* COUNTERFACTUAL.

convention In ordinary use, 'conventional behaviour' is what one calls accepted, especially artificial or customary, behaviour, sometimes resulting from explicit or tacit agreement. In current philosophical use, associated with David LEWIS, a convention for behaviour arises when it would be to everyone's advantage that actions be coordinated in any of a variety of arbitrary ways, and a convention is a rule that picks one of these ways. Thus, it is a (North American) convention that one drives to the right.

conventionalism *See* REALISM / ANTIREALISM, RIGHTS.

converse / obverse Terms of TRADITIONAL LOGIC. The converse of a statement is obtained by interchanging the subject and PREDICATE; thus, the converse of 'All pigs are sloppy eaters' is 'All sloppy eaters are pigs'. (You can see that conversion is not always a correct way to reason.) The obverse of a statement is obtained by changing 'No' to 'All' (or vice versa), or by changing 'Some...are' to 'Some...are not' (or vice versa); and by changing the predicate term to its COMPLEMENT. Thus, the obverse of 'No pigs are non-mammals' is 'All pigs are mammals', and the obverse of 'Some pigs are non-flying things' is 'Some pigs are not flying things'. All obversions are valid (*see* ARGUMENT).

Copernicus, Nicolaus *See* SCIENTISTS.

copula In TRADITIONAL LOGIC, the words that connect subject and PREDICATE **2**, such as 'is', 'are', 'are not', etc. ['COP-you-luh']

co-referential Two TERMS **2** — nouns or noun phrases — are co-referential when they REFER to exactly the same thing, or the same group of things. Coreferential terms do not always have the same meaning. In QUINE's example, 'animals with hearts' and 'animals with kidneys' are co-referential (because all and only animals with hearts are animals with kidneys), but these two terms have different meanings. The terms 'Mount Everest' and 'the tallest mountain on earth' are co-referential.

corporeal substance *See* SUBSTANCE.

correspondence theory of truth *See* TRUTH.

corrigibility *See* INCORRIGIBILITY.

cosmogony Theory about the origins of the universe. ['koz-MOG-uh-nee']

cosmological argument for God's existence *See* FIRST CAUSE ARGUMENT.

cosmology Philosophical or scientific theorizing about the COSMOS. Early philosophers often had ideas about where the cosmos came from, how it developed into the current form, and what its basic structure and laws were.

cosmos The universe as a whole, especially as the Greeks saw it. [sometimes spelled the way it's transliterated from Greek: 'kosmos']

counterexample An example intended to show that some general claim is false. Reasoning by counterexample is frequently a useful philosophical tactic for arguing against some position.

counterfactual A counterfactual (also called a 'counter-factual conditional' or a 'contrary-to-fact conditional') is a CONDITIONAL statement whose antecedent is false. In English we use the subjunctive in counterfactuals: 'If Fred were here, you wouldn't be doing that'. (This is properly said only if Fred isn't here.) One interesting and controversial area in modern LOGIC is concerned with figuring out what makes certain counterfactual conditionals true or false. A powerful and widely accepted way of understanding counterfactuals (associated with David LEWIS and others) uses the notion of POSSIBLE WORLDS: a counterfactual is true when the consequent is true in the nearest possible world (i.e., a world as much as possible like ours) in which the antecedent is true.

counterintuitive *See* INTUITION.

covering law A general LAW applying to a particular instance. The covering law theory of EXPLANATION says that a particular event is explained when one or more covering laws are given that (together with particular facts) IMPLY the event. For example, we can explain why a piece of metal rusted by appealing to the covering law that iron rusts when exposed to air and moisture, and the facts that this metal is iron, and was exposed to air and moisture.

creationism The religious doctrine that the world was created by a divine being, or that it owes its present form to divine agency. This term is frequently used to refer to the idea, associated with religious fundamentalism, that the world was created in exactly the way the Bible says it was, and more particularly to the idea that living things are the way they are because God designed them that way; this is opposed to the view that they developed through the natural processes of EVOLUTION.

criterion A test or standard for applying a word, or for the truth or falsity of some claim. This word is singular; its plural is 'criteria'.

Croce, Benedetto (1866-1952) Italian philosopher best known for his IDEALISTIC AESTHETICS. ['CROW-chay']

cube, reversing (Necker cube) *See* MÜLLER-LYER ILLUSION.

cultural relativism / absolutism *See* RELATIVISM / ABSOLUTISM.

curl The symbol '~', meaning 'not' or 'it is not the case that', also often called the TILDE.) (*see* SYMBOLS OF SENTENTIAL LOGIC).

cybernetics The science of systems of control and communication in animals and machines. See also ARTIFICIAL INTELLIGENCE. ['sigh-bur-NET-iks]

cynics / cynicism In ordinary talk, a cynic (someone who is cynical, who practices cynicism) is one who doubts the existence of human goodness and offers unpleasant reinterpretations of apparent examples of this, in which people are seen as less virtuous and more self-interested. The philosophical source for this word is the Cynics, ancient Greek philosophers who denounced the conventional methods of seeking happiness (possessions, family, religion, reputation, etc.), and advocated self-control, self-knowledge, and ASCETICISM. The best-known Greek Cynic was DIOGENES of Synope.

Cyrenaic Pertaining to the school of philosophy founded by ARISTIPPUS (in Cyrenaica), which held that pleasure was the only good in life.

D

Dante *See* WRITERS.

Darwin, Charles *See* SCIENTISTS.

Darwinism *See* EVOLUTION.

datum (Latin: "the given") Something GIVEN — an AS-SUMPTION or premise (*see* ARGUMENT) from which other claims may be DERIVED, or a starting point for knowledge. A SENSE-DATUM is that bit of internal experience we get when our senses reveal the world to us; some philosophers think that this is the basis for knowledge of the external world. The ARGUMENT FROM ILLUSION concludes that sense-data are what are always directly present to our minds when we use our senses; any information about externals must be inferred from these. ['Datum' is singular; plural 'data']

Davidson, Donald (b. 1917) American contemporary METAPHYSICIAN and philosopher of mind and of language.

decision matrix A table designed to display the features involved in various options and outcomes of a decision.

	Other confesses	Other doesn't confess
You confess	3 yrs in jail	1 yr in jail
You don't confess	4 yrs in jail	2 yrs in jail

For example, the decision matrix for the PRISONER'S DILEMMA is shown above.

Inside the four boxes are listed the consequences for you, given your action and that of the other prisoner.

de dicto / de re (Latin: "about what's said" / "about a thing") Usually a distinction concerning belief. A de re belief is a belief considered with respect to the actual thing that it's about. Thus, if someone mistakenly thinks that the moving thing in the sky he's looking at is a satellite, whereas it's actually a meteor, then he has the de re belief that a meteor is moving in the sky—more clearly: about that meteor, he believes it's moving in the sky above him. But he has the de dicto belief that a satellite is moving in the sky above him. ['day DIK-tow', 'day ray']

deduction / induction 1. In an outdated way of speaking, deduction is reasoning from the general to the particular, and induction is reasoning from the particular to the general. 2. Nowadays, this distinction between kinds of reasoning is made as follows: correct deductive reasoning is reasoning of the sort that if the premises (*see* ARGUMENT) are true, the conclusion must be true; whereas correct inductive reasoning supports the conclusion by showing only that it's more probably true. Examples:

Deduction: No pigs fly; Porky is a pig; therefore, Porky doesn't fly.

Induction: Porky, Petunia, and all the other pigs observed in a wide variety of circumstances don't fly; therefore no pigs fly.

These examples in fact fit definition 1; but here are examples of deduction according to definition 2 that do not fit definition 1:

No pigs fly; therefore all pigs are non-flying things.

Porky doesn't fly; Porky is a pig; therefore not all pigs fly.

The two main sorts of deductive logic are SENTEN-TIAL and QUANTIFIER LOGIC.

A common form of induction works by enumeration: as support for the conclusion that all p's are q's, one lists many examples of p's that are q's.

deep / surface structure The deep structure (or depth grammar) of a sentence is what linguists take to be its underlying structure at the basic level; this is contrasted with its surface structure (or surface grammar), which includes the characteristics that English teachers call 'grammar'. Thus, for example, the sentence 'Fred loves Zelda' has the same deep structure as 'Zelda is loved by Fred', though they have different surface structures. The study of deep structure is associated with Noam CHOMSKY, who is also known for his position that deep structure is an INNATELY provided feature of language.

definiens / definiendum A *definiendum* (Latin: "to be defined") is a word or phrase to be defined, and the definition is the definiens (Latin: "defining thing"). ['duh-fin-ee-ENS', 'duh-fin-ee-EN-dum']

definite / indefinite description A definite description is a term of the form 'the x', for example, 'the tallest man in Brazil'. A definite description can apply to at most one thing. An indefinite description, by contrast, can apply to any one of a number of things: 'a tall man'. A famous controversy involving definite descriptions concerns whether or not statements containing them have EXISTENTIAL IMPORT: that is, whether a sentence whose subject is a definite description that refers to nothing is therefore false. Consider the sentence 'The present king of France is bald'; does the fact that there is no present king of France make the sentence false? On RUSSELL's account of the definite description it does. STRAWSON, however, argues that the existence of the present king of France is merely PRESUPPOSED by this sentence, as the statement 'Fred has stopped beating his wife' presupposes that Fred had been beating her. If what the statement presupposes is not true, then the statement itself is neither true nor false.

defeasible Means 'defeatible', in the sense of 'capable of being overruled'. A driver's license confers a defeasible right to drive, for example, because under certain circumstances (e.g., when he is drunk) the holder of a valid license would nevertheless not be allowed to drive.

definition A procedure for giving the meaning of a word or phrase. There are various kinds of definition, including:

1. Verbal definition: using other words, giving synonymous words or phrases. This is the sort of definition found in dictionaries, but note that dictionaries often do more than merely this: they tell you, for example, facts about things to which the words refer—facts not definitionally associated with these words. Contrasted with:

2. Ostensive definition: done by giving examples. One might define the word 'green' by showing somebody a number of green things, or 'bird' by listing many different sorts of birds.

3. Functional definition: done by giving the typical use of the kind of thing, or its the typical cause-and-effect relations with other things (*see* FUNCTIONAL KIND)

4. Operational definition: done by giving a list of procedures or measurements for telling when the word applies.

5. Stipulative definition: determines the meaning of a freshly-coined term, or a new meaning for an old term. A precising definition stipulates a new meaning when the old one was insufficiently precise.

6. Recursive definition — *see* RECURSIVE.

7. Persuasive definition: When a word has acquired laudatory (or derogatory) overtones, it is sometimes redefined in accord with a speaker's evaluations. For example, even though the usual usage would count rock music as music, somebody who hated rock might refuse to call it that, because of the word's laudatory overtones. ("Nothing *that* loud is music!")

8. Emotive definition: The sort of definition appropriate for a word that has evaluative as well as descriptive implications. The definition of 'courage', for example, must say more than 'steadfastness in the face of danger', for this defines 'foolhardiness' as well. 'Courage' is steadfastness in the face of danger that one approves of.

9. Circular definition: *see* CIRCULAR REASONING / DEFINITION.

10. Definition by genus and species *see* GENUS / SPECIES. See also FAMILY RESEMBLANCE.

degrees of perfection argument for god's existence

This argument has been proposed in many different forms. Here's one:

Comparative terms describe degrees of approximation to superlative terms. So nothing would count as falling short of the superlative unless the superlative thing existed. Ordinary things are less than perfect, so there must be something completely perfect; and what is completely perfect is God.

An objection to this argument is that comparative terms do not imply the existence of a superlative instance. For example, the existence of people who are more or less stupid does not imply that someone exists who is maximally, completely, perfectly stupid.

deism A form of religious belief especially popular during the ENLIGHTENMENT. Deists believe that God produced the universe with its LAWS 3 of nature, but then left it alone to operate solely by these laws. This form of religious belief seems incompatible with some aspects of conventional religion, for example, with the notion of a loving God, or with the practice of prayer. VOLTAIRE, ROUSSEAU, and KANT were deists.

delusion *See* ILLUSION / HALLUCINATION / DELUSION.

demiurge An anglicised version of a Greek word that means 'craftsman'. In PLATO's *Timaeus* a Demiurge is pictured (perhaps just as a symbol or personification) as creating the universe, in conformity, as far as physical limitations allowed, with rationality and goodness. [sometimes the 'd' is capitalized when the word is thought to refer to God]

democracy That form of government whose actions are determined by the governed (or by their elected representatives). Often the meaning of this word is extended in a rather imprecise way to imply that democratic societies are EGALITARIAN, and respect individual rights.

Democritus (460?-?370 B.C.) Greek philosopher, originator of the theory of ATOMISM. He conceived of the world as consisting only of tiny indestructible atoms in motion, and empty space; the properties of these atoms determine their combinations and interactions, and explain the visible world of change. ['duh-MOCK-ruh-tus']

demonstrative / indexical A demonstrative term gets its REFERENCE by "pointing" — for example, 'this' in 'This is mine'. An indexical term similarly gets its reference from CONTEXT: the word 'today' changes its reference daily.

De Morgan, Augustus (1806-1871) British mathematician and logician, known for his work on LOGIC, the foundations of algebra, and the philosophy of mathematics.

De Morgan's laws The rules (named for Augustus DE MORGAN) for correct reasoning in SENTENTIAL LOGIC that state that one may reason correctly from a CONJUNCTION of NEGATIONS to the corresponding negated DISJUNCTION, or vice versa; or from a disjunction of negations to the corresponding negated conjunction or vice versa. It is easier to see this when put in symbolic form: it is correct to reason from a statement in any of these forms to its equivalent:

$(\sim p\ \&\ \sim q)$ is equivalent to $\sim (p \lor q)$

$(\sim p \lor \sim q)$ is equivalent to $\sim (p\ \&\ q)$

(*See* SYMBOLS OF SENTENTIAL LOGIC). Thus, for example, from 'It's not the case that it's raining or it's snowing' one may correctly derive 'It's not raining and it's not snowing'. ['duh MORE-gan']

denotation / connotation The denotation or REFERENCE of a word is what that word refers to — the things in the world that it "names." The connotation or sense of a word is, by contrast, its meaning. Thus, a word can have connotation but no denotation: 'unicorn' has meaning but no reference. (Synonymous with 'EXTENSION / INTENSION'.) Note that the philosophical use of 'connotation' is different from the ordinary one, in which it refers not to what a word means, but to more or less distant associations it has; for example, the word 'roses' may carry the connotation of romance to many people.

deontic Means 'having to do with OBLIGATION'. Deontic logic is that branch of MODAL LOGIC dealing with connections of sentences saying what one ought to do, must do, is permitted to do, etc.

deontology —*See* CONSEQUENTIALISM.

depth grammar *See* DEEP / SURFACE STRUCTURE.

de re *See* DE DICTO / DE RE

derivation A method for proving deductive validity, in which one writes down the premises, then moves to succeeding steps using accepted RULES OF INFERENCE, eventuating at the conclusion (*see* ARGUMENT). There are other methods of proof, for example, in SENTENTIAL LOGIC, the TRUTH-TABLE.

Derrida, Jacques (b. 1930) Algerian-born French philosopher, best-known of the post-STRUCTURALISTS. He sees his project as the "deconstruction" of our ideas and other cultural products to reveal their underlying ASSUMPTIONS 1, PRESUPPOSITIONS, and meanings.

Descartes, René (1596-1650) French philosopher and mathematician, the founder of MODERN PHILOSOPHY. Earlier SCHOLASTICISM saw the job of philosophy as analysing and proving truths revealed by religion;

Descartes' revolutionary view (which got him into trouble with the Church) was that philosophy can discover truth. His famous recipe for doing this is the method of systematic doubt (*see* CARTESIAN DOUBT); this is necessary to begin the search for the INDUBITABLE foundations for knowledge, the first of which is the truth of his own existence as a thinking (not a material) thing. Although he was a champion of MECHANISTIC thinking about the external material world, and in fact contributed substantially to the new science and mathematics, he was a DUALIST, and believed that minds are non-material. ['day-kart']

description, definite / indefinite *See* DEFINITE / INDEFINITE DESCRIPTION.

description, knowledge by *See* KNOWLEDGE BY ACQUAINTANCE / BY DESCRIPTION.

descriptive ethics *See* NORMATIVE / DESCRIPTIVE.

design, argument from *See* TELEOLOGICAL ARGUMENT FOR GOD'S EXISTENCE.

designator, rigid / flaccid *See* RIGID / FLACCID DESIGNATOR.

determinism The view that every event has previous causes, so that given its causes, each event must have existed in the form it does. There is some debate about how (and whether) this view can be JUSTIFIED **1**. The view that at least some events are not fully caused is called 'indeterminism'. Determinism is usually a PRESUPPOSITION of science; KANT thought it was NECESSARY; but quantum physics says that it is false. One of the main areas of concern about determinism arises when it is considered in connection with FREE WILL.

deterrence Preventing future occurrences of undesirable acts by punishing present instances, or by threat of PUNISHMENT. This is one of the JUSTIFICATIONS 1 philosophers give for punishment. Thus, for example, one may try to justify jailing criminals by claiming that such a practice will discourage them and others from future crime. Nuclear deterrence attempts to prevent a future nuclear attack by threatening massive retaliation. The moral status of deterrence is controversial. Preventing nuclear war is of course a good thing, but is nuclear deterrence justified, given that it involves the willingness to go through with really horrible retaliation?

Dewey, John (1859-1953) American philosopher associated with PRAGMATISM and INSTRUMENTALISM, with the notion of WARRANTED ASSERTIBILITY in the explanation of truth, and with educational theory and reform.

diachronic *See* SYNCHRONIC / DIACHRONIC.

dialectic This word stems from a Greek root meaning 'conversation', but it has come to have many meanings in philosophy. Some of the more important of these are: **1.** The method of philosophical argument used by the PRESOCRATICS and SOCRATES, typically refuting opponents' positions by drawing out unacceptable consequences of those positions (*see* SOCRATIC METHOD). **2.** For PLATO, as for his predecessors, dialectic is a process of question-and- answer discussion, but Plato emphasized that this was aimed at discovering general and unchanging truths. **3.** ARISTOTELIAN dialectic is reasoning from probable premises. **4.** HEGELIAN dialectic is a process of reasoning starting with disagreement and argument, proceeding through revision toward greater sophistication and adequacy, and aiming at agreement. Hegel thought that this also described the processes of nature and history; his view is often described as holding that change takes place when some thing (the thesis) and its opposite (the antithesis) interact to produce a new unity (the synthesis), which becomes the thesis of another change. Hegelian dialectical logic emphasizes the processes things undergo, rather than the LOGICAL FORM of sentences, and denies the universal validity of the so-called LAWS OF THOUGHT.

dialectical materialism / idealism These theories of historical change combine a DIALECTICAL **4.** theory of change with historical materialism and idealism, respectively (*see* HISTORICAL MATERIALISM / IDEALISM). Dialectical materialism is closely associated with MARXIST thought, in which the historical process is understood in terms of a process of conflict and resolution between opposing material (i.e., economic) forces and entities in society. This term is also more broadly used to refer to Marxist-LENINIST philosophy and political IDEOLOGY in general. Dialectical idealism, associated with HEGEL, thinks of history in terms of dialectical processes involving the ABSOLUTE Spirit.

Diderot, Denis (1713-1784) French literary and philosophical writer. An important figure in the French ENLIGHTENMENT, known for his NATURALISTIC views and his MATERIALISM and DETERMINISM. ['dee-der-oh']

difference, method of *See* MILL'S METHODS.

differentia *See* GENUS / SPECIES.

dilemma People often use this word inaccurately to mean any sort of problem. Its correct use refers to that sort of problem in which one has a choice between two unpleasant alternatives (called 'horns of the dilemma'). A moral dilemma is a forced choice between two incompatible but apparently binding OBLIGATIONS, or between two morally unacceptable alternatives—for example, when telling the truth would hurt someone, but lying would also be wrong. Philosophers sometimes use this word to refer to a kind of ARGUMENT that forces the opponent to choose between two possibilities (*see also* CONSTRUCTIVE DILEMMA).

ding an sich *See* THING-IN-ITSELF.

Dilthey, Wilhelm (1833-1911) German philosopher, known for his analyses of nature and of the methodology of human studies.

Diogenes of Sinope (412?-323 B.C.) Greek philosopher associated with the CYNICS. Known for his advocacy of a self-contained unconventional life. ['dy-AH-jen-eez']

Dionysian *See* APOLLONIAN / DIONYSIAN.

disanalogy *See* ANALOGY.

disconfirmation *See* CONFIRMATION / DISCONFIRMATION.

disjunction A sentence contstructed out of two sentences connected by 'or'. The sentence 'It's raining or it's snowing' can be seen to be composed of the disjunction of the two sentences 'It's raining' and 'It's snowing'. Two sentences connected in this way are called 'disjuncts'. It is often thought that there are two sorts of disjunction ambiguously expressed by 'or' in English. (1) The exclusive disjunction is true when one of the disjuncts is true and the other false, and false otherwise (when both are true, or when both are false). (2) The inclusive disjunction is true when one or both of the disjuncts are true, and false only when both of the disjuncts are false.

Suppose, then, that both snow and rain are coming down at once. Is the sentence 'It's snowing or it's raining' true? If this 'or' is taken to be inclusive, it's true; if exclusive, it's false. Standardly in SENTENTIAL LOGIC, the wedge, also called the vee (∨) symbolizes the inclusive disjunction (*see* SYMBOLS OF SENTENTIAL LOGIC).

disjunctive syllogism A form of reasoning using a DISJUNCTION as one premise (*see* ARGUMENT), and the negation of one of the disjuncts as the other premise; the other disjunct follows as conclusion. For example:

Either we'll go to the zoo or we'll stay home.

But we won't stay home.

Therefore we'll go to the zoo.

disposition A property whose presence or absence would be manifested — would make an observable difference — only under certain conditions. Brittleness is a dispositional property: to say that something is brittle is to say that it will shatter if struck with sufficient force. Two pieces of metal, only one of which is brittle, may seem identical. The difference will be revealed only if both are struck.

distributive justice *See* JUSTICE.

distributively *See* COLLECTIVELY / DISTRIBUTIVELY.

disvalue The opposite of 'value'. Something has disvalue not when it merely lacks value, but rather when it is positively bad. Pain has disvalue.

divine attributes The characteristics often thought to be
true of God. These include OMNIPOTENCE, OMNIS-
CIENCE, and BENEVOLENCE.

doctrine of acts and omissions *See* ACTS / OMISSIONS.

dogma A system of belief, especially one laid down officially and required by a religion. Thus, this word has also
come to mean anything someone believes merely on
authority, without reason, especially when stated ar-
rogantly and intolerantly.

dominance 1. The ordinary meaning of this word is 'exer-
cising the most influence or control', and in this sense,
dominance is a concern of ethics of personal relations,
and political philosophy. **2.** In a technical sense used in
decision theory, one choice is said to be dominant if it
has better features or consequences than the alternatives, whatever happens. The dominance principle tells
you to pick the alternative that dominates. Of course,
sometimes there is no such alternative, so this is of
limited applicability. Other principles of decision theory
are the MAXIMIN principle, and the principle that one
should maximize EXPECTED UTILITY.

Dostoyevsky, Fyodor Mikhailovich — *See* WRITERS.

dot The symbol '·', meaning 'and' (*see* SYMBOLS OF SEN-
TENTIAL LOGIC).

double-aspect theory *See* DUAL ASPECT THEORY.

double effect The doctrine of double effect holds that, although it is always wrong to use a bad means to a good
end (*see* END / MEANS), one may act to bring about a
good result when also knowingly bringing about bad
results, under the following conditions: (1) The bad

result is not caused by the good result—both are caused by the action (thus 'double effect'); (2) there's no way of getting the good result without the bad; (3) the good result is so good that it's worth accepting the bad one. For example, a dentist is allowed to drill, and thus cause some pain (the bad result) for the sake of dental improvements (the good result), since these conditions hold—most notably (1): the pain doesn't cause the improvement—both are results of the drilling. This principle is associated with Catholic morality, and has been applied most frequently in contexts of medical ethics. It is disputed by some philosophers, who sometimes argue that the distinction between double effect and bad means / good end is artificial and not morally relevant.

doubt To doubt something can mean either to be uncertain or undecided about it, or to believe that it is false. When philosophical SCEPTICS present arguments for doubting ordinarily accepted statements, they may attempt to show that one should be uncertain or undecided about them, or should actually think they are false. But often the sceptic wants to show that the ordinarily accepted statement can't be justified—that it is without foundation.

doubt, Cartesian *See* CARTESIAN DOUBT.

dual aspect theory A theory (associated with SPINOZA and others) that mind and body are just different aspects of, different ways of looking at, the same SUBSTANCE or thing; so it's a form of monism (*see* DUALISM / MONISM / PLURALISM). Also called the 'double aspect theory'.

dualism / monism / pluralism All three are views on the basic kind(s) of things that exist. Dualists hold that there are two sorts of things, neither of which can be understood in terms of the other. Often 'dualism' refers particularly to the view in philosophy of mind in which the two are the mental and the physical (*see* INTERACTIONISM, OCCASIONALISM, and PARALLELISM for particular varieties). Other sorts of dualism distinguish the visible and invisible, the actual and the possible, God and the universe, etc. Monists believe in only one ultimate kind of thing, and pluralists in many. To be a pluralist about value is to believe that there are many incompatible, but equally valid, value systems.

duck-rabbit *See* MÜLLER-LYER ILLUSION.

dubitability *See* INDUBITABILITY / DUBITABILITY.

Duhem, Pierre *See* SCIENTISTS.

dunce Not a philosophical term, but you might be amused to know that it's derived from the name of DUNS SCOTUS (his followers were called 'dunces' by their opponents).

Duns Scotus, John (1265?-1308) Scottish theologian and philosopher; interests in THEOLOGY and METAPHYSICS.

Durkheim, Emile (1858-1917) *See* SCIENTISTS.

duty *See* OBLIGATION.

dystopia *See* UTOPIA.

E

Eddington, Arthur *see* SCIENTISTS.

Edwards, Jonathan (1703-1757) American puritan THEOLOGIAN.

effect, double *See* DOUBLE EFFECT.

efficient / formal / material / final causes Aristotle's "four CAUSES": **1.** The efficient cause of something: what brings it into existence **2.** The formal cause: its abstract structure—its "blueprint." **3.** The material cause: what it's made of **4.** The final cause: its purpose or aim. Aristotle clearly did not mean by 'cause' what we do: perhaps his four causes should be understood as the four basic kinds of characteristics that things have, which are useful in categorizing them and explaining what they're like and how they work.

egalitarianism The view that people are equal—that they are entitled to equal rights and treatment in society.

ego, empirical / transcendental *See* EMPIRICAL / TRANSCENDENTAL EGO.

egoism, ethical / psychological Psychological egoism is the position that people in fact act only in their own IN-TERESTS. If you think this is true, be careful that your belief is not merely an empty thought. It's sometimes argued that even the most generous act is done for the doer's own satisfaction; but this might simply be a way of saying that even the most generous act is motivated—

something nobody would deny. If someone is motivated to act for others' benefit, and gets satisfaction from those actions, this shows that psychological egoism is not universally true. Ethical egoism is the position that I (or people in general) ought to act only in my (their) own interests. 'Egotism' is sometimes used synonymously, but precise speakers tend to use 'egotism' to mean the tendency to speak or write of oneself too much, or too boastfully. ['EE-go-ism' or 'EH-go-ism'] See also: SELFISHNESS, RATIONAL SELF-INTEREST.

eidos *See* PLATONIC FORMS.

Einstein, Albert —*see* SCIENTISTS.

élan vital *See* VITALISM.

elements The elements of something are its basic components. The Greeks believed that all physical things were composed of four basic elements: earth, air, fire, and water. Nowadays, of course, we believe in different elements, and there are many more of them; neither are they basic (they can be ANALYZED into sub-atomic components).

eliminativism *See* MATERIALISM.

emergent properties These are characteristics had by a group of things considered as a whole, but not by the things that make up the group. A group of people, for example, can have the property of electing an official, while no particular person does this. We can understand what it is to elect an official in terms of the voting of individuals; but a stronger and more controversial version of emergentism holds that emergent properties are those that can't be ANALYZED into different properties of individual components.

Emerson, Ralph Waldo *See* WRITERS

emotivism A position in meta-ethics (*see* NORMATIVE /
DESCRIPTIVE), that holds that ethical utterances are to
be understood not as statements of fact that are either
true or false, but rather as expressions of approval or
disapproval, and invitations to the listener to have the
same reactions. Expressions of approval don't state
facts: when I express my liking of ice cream by saying
"Yum!" what I'm saying is neither true nor false. Neither
is what I say when I urge you to try some. HUME might be
construed as holding a form of emotivism; in this century, the position is associated with A. J. AYER and the
American philosopher C(harles) L(eslie) Stevenson
(1908-1975).

empathy *See* SYMPATHY / EMPATHY.

Empedocles (490?-430 B.C.) Greek philosopher; his
poem "On Nature" contains elaborate theories of the
origin and constitution of the universe.

empirical This means having to do with sense-experience
and experiment. Empirical knowledge is knowledge we
get through experience of the world; thus it is *a posteriori*
(*see A PRIORI / A POSTERIORI*). An empirical CONCEPT is
one that is not INNATE; it can be developed only through
experience.

empirical / transcendental ego (In Latin, '*ego*' means
"I.") The ego is the "I" — the self. This distinction is
KANT's. The EMPIRICAL ego is the collection of charac-
teristics and mental events that we can sense, perhaps by
INTROSPECTION; the TRANSCENDENTAL ego is what
unifies — what *has* — these characteristics, perhaps a
mental SUBSTANCE we can't sense (*see* also BUNDLE
THEORY).

empiricism The position (usually contrasted with RATIONALISM) that all our CONCEPTS and substantive knowledge come from experience. Empiricists deny that there are INNATE concepts. While they grant that certain kinds of trivial knowledge (of CONCEPTUAL, ANALYTIC, and LOGICAL TRUTHS) can be gained by reason alone, independently of experience, they deny the existence of the synthetic (*see* ANALYTIC / SYNTHETIC) *A PRIORI*. ARISTOTLE is perhaps the founder of empiricism; the position is most strongly associated with EPICURUS among the Greeks. The classical MODERN empiricists were LOCKE, BERKELEY, and HUME. MILL was a strong empiricist. The view has been an important influence on contemporary ANALYTIC PHILOSOPHY. ['em-PEER-uh-sism', 'em-PEER-uh-kl']

empiricist *See* EMPIRICISM.

empty set *See* SET.

end in itself 1. Something sought for its own sake; an IN-TRINSIC good. 2. Someone is seen as an end in him / her-self when that person's aims are seen as having value just because they are that person's aims. Treating someone as an end in him / herself is respecting his / her aims, and not thinking of, or using, that person merely as a means to your aims. A central principle of KANT's ethics is the necessity of treating others as ends-in-themselves, and not as means only.

ends / means A long-standing controversy in ethics is whether one might be permitted to use bad means to a good end: does the end justify the means? For example, is it permitted to lie to someone if everyone will be better off in the long run as a result? The distinction between ends and means parallels the distinction between intrinsic and extrinsic goods — *see* INTRINSIC / INHERENT / IN-STRUMENTAL / EXTRINSIC. See also: DOUBLE EFFECT, CATEGORICAL / HYPOTHETICAL IMPERATIVE.

Enlightenment A cultural and philosophical movement of the seventeenth and eighteenth centuries. Its chief features were a belief in rationality and scientific method, and a tendency to reject traditional religion and other traditions.

en soi See IN-ITSELF / FOR-ITSELF.

entailment One sentence entails another when the second follows logically from the first — that is, when the argument with the first as premise and the second as conclusion is valid (*see* ARGUMENT).

entelechy A non-material force or purpose that is supposed to cause something to come into existence. In ARISTOTLE, also the state of achieved potential that things aim at (*see* EFFICIENT / FORMAL / MATERIAL / FINAL CAUSES 4). ['en-TEL-uh-kee']

entertain To entertain a PROPOSITION is to consider it without necessarily believing it.

enthymeme An argument with some steps left unstated but understood. 'All pigs are sloppy eaters, so Porky is a sloppy eater' is an enthymeme, leaving unsaid 'Porky is a pig'. ['EN-thuh-meem']

entity A thing, an existent being.

entities, hypothetical / theoretical See THEORETICAL ENTITIES.

enumerative inductive inference See DEDUCTION / IN-DUCTION.

Epictetus (60?-117) Greek STOIC; his views emphasized duty and inner freedom. ['ep-ik-TEE-tus']

Epicurus (of Samos) (342?-?270 B.C.) Greek philosopher known for his MATERIALIST, ATOMIST, and DETERMINIST views, and for his position that the good life was one based on pleasure. ['ep-uh-CURE-us']

epicureanism The ordinary use of the word 'epicurean', meaning devoted to pleasure, especially that of fine food, has distant connections to its philosophical use, in which it refers to the philosophy of EPICURUS and his followers. Chief tenets are an emphasis on the visible world (as opposed to the world imagined by religion or many philosophies), and the advocation of calmness of mind. ['ep-uh-kew-REE-an-ism']

Epimenides' paradox *See* LIAR'S PARADOX.

epiphenomenalism A variety of DUALISM in which mental events are just "by-products" of physical ones: physical events cause mental ones, but not vice versa. As an analogy, think of the noise your car makes: it's caused by the mechanical goings-on inside, but it has no effect on them. ['ep-ee-feh-NOM-in-al-ism']

epistemic Having to do with knowledge. Epistemic logic is that branch of MODAL LOGIC dealing with relations between sentences involving 'knows', 'believes', etc. ['ep-is-TEE-mik' or 'ep-is-TEH-mik']

epistemology Theory of knowledge: one of the main branches of philosophy. Among the central questions studied here are: What is the difference between knowledge and mere belief? Is all (or any) knowledge based on sense-perception? How, in general, are our knowledge-claims justified? ['eh-piss-teh-MOL-uh-jee']

E proposition *See* A / E / I / O PROPOSITIONS.

equivalence *See* BICONDITIONAL.

equivocation An ambiguous word, or a shift in the course of speaking or reasoning from one meaning of a word to another. Equivocation is sometimes used to mislead; and sometimes it results in faulty reasoning (the FALLACY of equivocation). An example, which equivocates on the word 'law':

The existence of any law shows that there is a law-maker.

The law of gravity was not made by humans.

Therefore there must be a non-human law-maker — God. ['ih-kwiv-uh-KAY-shun']

Erasmus, Desiderius *See* WRITERS.

eros *See* AGAPE.

eschatological Having to do with "the last matters" — especially, in Christian thought, with death, the end of the world, the Last Judgement, Heaven, Hell, and the significance of these for our present lives. Don't confuse this word with 'scatological', which means something quite different. ['es-kat-uh-LODGE-i-cal']

e.s.p *See* PARANORMAL PHENOMENA.

essence / accident Those characteristics of something that it must have in order to be what it is, or the kind of thing it is. It is essential, for example, for a tree to be a plant — if something was not a plant, it could not be a tree. By contrast, a tree that in fact is thirty-three meters high could still be a tree if it weren't thirty-three meters high; thus this characteristic is accidental. (Note that 'accident' and 'accidental' don't have their ordinary meanings in this philosophical use.) Some philosophers think that the essence / accident distinction does not concern the real characteristics of something, but is only a consequence of the words we apply to them: being a plant is said to be an essential characteristic of a tree only because it's part of the definition of 'tree'. But essentialist philosophers believe in real, objective essences.

essential / accidental quality / property / characteristic *See* ESSENCE / ACCIDENT.

esse est percipi (Latin: "to be is to be perceived") This slogan is associated with BERKELEY, who thought that nothing existed except perceptions in a mind. See also PHENOMENALISM. ['essay est pur-KIP-ee']

esthetics *See* AESTHETICS.

eternal return The doctrine that every event and series of events has occurred, and will occur, over and over again, identical in every detail, an infinite number of times. This was held by a number of ANCIENT, MEDIEVAL, and nineteenth-century philosophers. Also known as 'eternal recurrence'.

ether The invisible "stuff" formerly thought to permeate everything, including apparently empty space, supposed to be the medium for apparent ACTION-AT-A-DISTANCE. ['EE-thur'; sometimes spelled 'aether']

ethical cognitivism / noncognitivism *See*   COGNITIVISM / NONCOGNITIVISM.

ethical Darwinism *See* EVOLUTION.

ethical egoism *See* EGOISM.

ethical naturalism / supernaturalism / nonnaturalism
Those who think that the ethical words like 'good' and 'right' may be defined in terms of natural properties (the ordinary properties of the physical world) are ethical naturalists. For example, some ethical naturalists think that 'the right act' means 'the act that produces the most happiness'. Ethical supernaturalism is the view that ethical properties really are properties having to do with the supernatural or divine: for example, the view that calling an action good is the same as saying that it conforms to the will of God. Nonnaturalists deny that ethical words are equivalent in meaning to words that name the natural (or supernatural) world, though good things may as a matter of fact share some physical properties. They claim that ethical properties are basic properties on their own, not really properties in some other realm.

ethical relativism / absolutism *See* RELATIVISM / ABSOLUTISM.

ethics *See* MORALITY.

ethics, normative / descriptive *See* NORMATIVE / DESCRIPTIVE.

ethics, teleological *See* TELEOLOGY.

ethnocentric Someone is ethnocentric who regards the views or characteristics of his / her own race or culture as the only correct or important ones.

Etiology *See* AETIOLOGY.

eudaemonia (Greek: "living well") Since ARISTOTLE thought that the happy life was the good life, this word might be taken to mean 'happiness', particularly the complex and long-lasting kind of happiness that Aristotle had in mind. His position can be called "eudaemonism" — the view that this is the real aim of life. ['you-duh-MO-nee-ah']

Euler's diagram *See* VENN DIAGRAM.

euthanasia Euthanasia is mercy-killing, the intentional killing of someone, presumably for his own good, when his life is judged not to be worth continuing, often when that person is suffering from an untreatable, fatal illness causing horrible unavoidable pain or suffering. Voluntary euthanasia is killing done at the expressed wish of that person; this wish is not expressed in the case of involuntary euthanasia (for example, when the person has mentally deteriorated beyond the point of being able to express, or perhaps even to have, coherent wishes). Passive euthanasia involves refraining from providing life-prolonging treatment to someone suffering from a fatal condition; active euthanasis is killing, for example, by administering a fatal injection. Ethical opinion is deeply divided concerning euthanasia. Often those who argue in favour of its permissibility would accept it only when voluntary, and / or only when passive. ['you-tha-NAY-zee-ah' or 'you-tha-NAY-zha']

evil genius As part of his technique of CARTESIAN DOUBT, DESCARTES imagined that a powerful but evil spirit could be systematically fooling us about everything we thought we knew. (The French term for this evil genius is *'malin genie'*, roughly, 'ma-lah zhay-nec'.)

evil, problem of *See* PROBLEM OF EVIL.

evolution Broadly speaking, any process by which something gradually changes into a different, usually more complex, form. Most often used to refer to theories of change of kinds of living things, especially to the view, nowadays, held by almost all biologists that living creatures owe their present state of complex adaptation to their environment to a long natural process in which inherited characteristics varied at random; the characteristics that were more adaptive in the bearers' environment allowed those bearers to survive and reproduce, passing those characteristics on. This scientific THEORY is associated with Darwin (*see* SCIENTISTS), so it is sometimes called Darwinism; his name is also associated with some moral and social theories (ethical and social Darwinism) that hold that the good can be identified with the more evolved, and that social policies ought to be based on the furthering of evolution (for example, by refraining from interfering with "natural" processes, and allowing those with less "fit" genetic endowment to die off). Darwin was not a social or ethical Darwinist.

excluded middle, law of the *See* 'law of the excluded middle', in LAWS OF THOUGHT.

exclusive or / disjunction See DISJUNCTION.

exhaustive See MUTUALLY EXCLUSIVE / JOINTLY EXHAUSTIVE.

existence The subject of many different philosophical problems, for example: Is all that exists mental in nature (see IDEALISM) or physical (see MATERIALISM)? Are we justified in believing in things—for example, THEORETICAL ENTITIES or UNIVERSALS—that we don't perceive (see REALISM)? This word is sometimes misspelled 'existance'. Don't do that.

existential The adjectival form of the word 'existence'and the root of the term 'EXISTENTIALISM'. For some of its uses *see* the following entries. ['eggs-iss-TEN-shul']

existential anguish The horrible feeling the EXISTEN-TIALISTS suppose we have when confronted with our own complete and irremovable FREEDOM **1.** and RESPONSIBILITY.

existential import Said to be true of a sentence when it ASSERTS or IMPLIES or PRESUPPOSES the existence of something. If we take the sentence, 'All unicorns have horns' to have existential import, it implies that unicorns exist, so it is false.

existentialism A school of philosophy developed largely in twentieth-century France and Germany, closely associated with SARTRE and HEIDEGGER. Although existentialists have had things to say about many areas of philosophy, they are best known for their views on FREEDOM **1.** and RESPONSIBILITY. They tend to believe that we are totally free — that we are never caused to act by environment, heredity, or personality; and thus that we individually create all our decisions and values (the only source for ethical obligation) and are responsible for all our actions. ['eggs-iss-TEN-shul-ism']

existential quantifier See SYMBOLS OF QUANTIFIER LOGIC.

expected utility The expected utility of an ACTION is calculated by multiplying the UTILITY of each possible result of that action by its PROBABILITY, and adding up the results. For example, consider this betting game: you get $10 if a random draw from a deck of cards is a spade; and you pay $4 if it's any other suit. Assuming the utility of each dollar is 1, to calculate the expected utility of this game we add:

.25 (probability of a spade) x 10 (the utility if it's a spade) +

.75 (the probability of a non-spade) x -4 (the utility of a non-spade).

Since (.25 x 10) + (.75 x -3) = (2.5 3) = -.5, the game thus has an expected utility of -.5; not playing at all has an expected utility of 0. One (controversial) theory for rational decision-making advocates maximizing expected utility, so you should not play this game. (But if you just enjoy gambling, this has to be figured in too, and might make it worthwhile.) *See also* MINIMAX, DOMINANCE.

experience, mystical / religious *See:* MYSTICAL EXPERIENCE ARGUMENT FOR GOD'S EXISTENCE, MYSTICISM.

experimentum crucis (Latin: "crucial experiment") This is an experiment whose outcome would provide a central or conclusive test for the truth or falsity of some position or scientific HYPOTHESIS. ['ex-pair-uh-MEN-tum CROO-chis']

explanans / explanandum An explanandum (Latin: "to be explained") is something that is being explained: what does the explaining is the explanans (Latin: "explaining thing"). ['ex-pluh-NANS', 'ex-pluh-NAN-dum']

explanation An explanation answers the question 'Why?' and provides understanding; perhaps it also provides us with the abilities to control, and to predict (and RETRODICT) the world. This is fairly vague, and philosophers have tried to provide theories of explanation—to give a general account of how explanations work, and what makes some good and some bad. One important account is the COVERING LAW model. One (but only one) sort of explanation is CAUSAL: one explains something by saying what its causes are. Sometimes, instead, we explain by telling what something is made of, or by giving reasons for human ACTIONS (*but see* REASONS / CAUSES), as in some explanations in history.

extension / intension [Note the 's' in 'intension'; be careful not to confuse 'intensional' with 'INTENTIONAL'.] **1.** Sometimes 'extension' is used synonymously with 'denotation' and 'intension' with 'connotation' (*see* DENOTATION / CONNOTATION). Thus the extension of a term or a PREDICATE is the SET of things to which that term or predicate applies (*see* COEXTENSIVE). **2.** An extensional CONTEXT is a referentially transparent context; an intensional CONTEXT is a referentially opaque context (*see* OPAQUE / TRANSPARENT). An extensional logic is a TRUTH-FUNCTIONAL logic. **3.** The extension of something is its dimensions in space. Having extension is characteristic of things composed of extended SUBSTANCE, also known as 'physical substance'. Mental substance is unextended — it has no spatial dimensions. (In this sense, 'extensional' does not contrast with a corresponding sense of 'intensional'.)

extrasensory perception *See* PARANORMAL PHENOMENA.

extrinsic *See* INTRINSIC / INHERENT / INSTRUMENTAL / EXTRINSIC.

F

facticity An EXISTENTIALIST term meaning the sum of facts true of a person and his / her world. For HEIDEGGER, facticity is our world seen as not of our creation, something we involuntarily find ourselves inserted into.

faith Belief in something (usually God) despite lack of adequate evidence, or even in the face of contrary evidence. In religious circles, 'faith' also often refers to love of and trust in God, and other attitudes thought religiously appropriate.

faith, bad / good *See* BAD FAITH / GOOD FAITH / AUTHENTICITY / INAUTHENTICITY.

fallacy A fallacy is an ARGUMENT of a type that may seem correct to someone but in fact is not. (Thus, not just any mistaken argument should be called 'fallacious'.) Formal fallacies are mistakes in reasoning that spring from mistakes in LOGICAL FORM; an example is an argument involving ASSERTING THE CONSEQUENT. Informal fallacies spring instead from ambiguities in meaning or grammar, or from psychological tendencies to be convinced by reasons that are not good reasons. A synonym for 'fallacy' is 'paralogism'. Fallacies defined in this dictionary are *AD BACULUM*, *AD HOC* reasoning, *AD HOMINEM*, *AD IGNORANTIUM*, AFFIRMING THE CONSEQUENT, AMPHIBOLE, COMPOSITION, misplaced CONCRETENESS, EQUIVOCATION, FALSE CAUSE, GAMBLER'S FALLACY, GENETIC FALLACY, *IGNORATIO ELENCHI*, MODAL FALLACY, Monte Carlo fallacy (*see* GAMBLER'S

FALLACY), NATURALISTIC FALLACY, PATHETIC FAL-
LACY, *post hoc ergo propter hoc* (*see* FALSE CAUSE).

false cause Mistaken reasoning about the cause of something. We sometimes misidentify x as the cause of y because x happened before y (for example, if someone
thought that a falling barometer caused it to rain); this
sort of reasoning is called 'post hoc ergo propter hoc'
(Latin: "after that, therefore because of that," ['post
hock AIR-go PROP-tur hock']. And sometimes when
two things tend to occur together because they are both
caused by a third, we mistakenly think that one causes
another.

false, logically *See* LOGICAL TRUTH / FALSEHOOD.

falsifiability *See* VERIFIABILITY.

falsification *See* CONFIRMATION / DISCONFIRMATION /
VERIFICATION / FALSIFICATION.

family resemblance By ANALOGY with the ways members of a family resemble each other, this is the sort of
similarity that things classified into certain groups share:
each shares characteristics with many but not all of the
others, and there are no NECESSARY OR SUFFICIENT
CONDITIONS for belonging in that classification. WIT-
TGENSTEIN argued that many of our CONCEPTS are fami-
ly-resemblance concepts, so they cannot be defined by
necessary and sufficient conditions. His best-known example is the concept of a game.

Fārābī, Al- (more fully Abu-Nasr Muhammad al-Farabi;
Latin names Alfarabius or Avennasar) (873?-950)
Philosopher of Turkish origin, considered one of the
greatest Muslim philosophers. His views were based on

PLATO and ARISTOTLE, modified by the doctrines of Islam.

Faraday, Michael *See* SCIENTISTS.

fascism A form of government characterized by an extremely strong and AUTHORITARIAN right-wing, nationalistic, and often racist government in which the INTERESTS of the state supersede any individual's interests; thus fascist states deny individual RIGHTS and FREEDOMS 2. With a capital 'F', it refers to the government of Mussolini's Italy; with a lower-case 'f', it characterizes Nazi Germany and some other governments. Most of the philosophers known to us today were hostile to fascism; one exception was HEIDEGGER. ['FASH-ism']

fatalism The position that our futures are inevitable, whatever we do—that events are "fated" to happen. It's important to distinguish this from DETERMINISM, which claims merely that our futures are determined. A determinist who is not a fatalist thinks that our futures are not inevitable—they depend on what we do.

feel Some philosophy students express their philosophical positions by saying, "I feel that..." This suggests that they regard their positions as mere feelings—vague attitudes that can't be defended and shouldn't be trusted. Don't be so modest. Philosophers are supposed to make clear claims and argue for them, so it's better to say "I think that..." or "I believe that...," or just to make an ASSERTION unmodified by any of these phrases.

felicific calculus BENTHAM thought that the best ACTION was the one that produced the greatest happiness for the greatest number of people (*see* UTILITARIANISM), so he proposed that we determine what was right by quantifying the amounts of happiness produced by each result of an action, adding them up, and comparing this sum to the sum for other possible actions (*see* EXPECTED UTILITY). 'Felicific' means 'having to do with happiness', so this process is called the 'felicific CALCULUS'; also sometimes called the 'felicity', 'pleasure-pain', 'HEDONIC', or 'happiness calculus'. ['fel-uh-SIF-ik']

feminism The name of various philosophical — especially ethical, social, and political — THEORIES and movements that see elements of our society as unjust to and exploitative of women, and which advocate their change. Feminists often advocate equality under the law, and equal economic status, especially in employment opportunity, for women; but many go further, arguing in favour of preferential treatment for women to counteract past injustices. Sometimes they extend their analysis, finding male bias in many basic parts of our personal, social, and intellectual lives.

Fichte, Johann Gottlieb (1762-1814) German philosopher, student of KANT. Knowledge for him is the product of a free self-determining creative intellect; a central notion is the "ABSOLUTE" — identified with God, and containing the moral order of the universe. ['FICH-tuh', where the 'ch' is a throaty hiss, as in the German word 'ICH']

fideism The position that knowledge, especially of a religious sort, depends on faith or REVELATION.

final cause *See* EFFICIENT / FORMAL / MATERIAL / FINAL CAUSES.

first cause argument for God's existence Here's one version of this argument:

Every natural event has a preceding cause; tracing this CAUSAL CHAIN back in time would lead to an infinite series, without any start, if there were no first, supernatural cause. But an infinite series of this sort is impossible—something without a start doesn't exist. So there must have been a first, supernatural cause (an "UNMOVED MOVER"): God.

This argument is often criticized by questioning its ASSUMPTION that an infinite series is impossible. It is sometimes thought that the ancient Greeks, for whom the notion of infinity was unthinkable, found this assumption plausible; but we now are able to think about infinity, and need not accept it.

first mover *See* UNMOVED MOVER.

first principles The INDUBITABLE assumptions from which other truths are derived; ASSUMPTIONS, AXIOMS, POSITS. Some philosophers think these must be the starting point for any reliable system of belief. *See also* FOUNDATIONALISM.

five ways St. THOMAS AQUINAS's five arguments for God's existence:

(1) Things are moving and changing; thus there must have been a FIRST CAUSE.

(2) Things need causes to exist; thus there must have been a first cause.

(3) Things are contingent (*see* NECESSARY / CONTINGENT), so there must be something that's necessary.

(4) Things fall short of perfection; therefore something perfect exists. (*See* DEGREES OF PERFECTION ARGUMENT).

(5) Things are orderly and collectively tend toward a universal aim; thus there must be an intelligent Orderer (*See* TELEOLOGICAL ARGUMENT).

flaccid designator *See* RIGID / FLACCID DESIGNATOR

Folk Psychology The name given by some philosophers of mind to our ordinary everyday ways of thinking about people and their minds, seen as a THEORY committed to the existence of beliefs, desires, personality traits, etc. Some philosophers argue that folk psychology fails various tests for good scientific theories (not merely because there is not much of the sort of observation and experiment we would expect in good science), and so, like other primitive belief-systems (e.g., astrology, belief in witches) it should be replaced by a more rigorous science of the mind not committed to the existence of beliefs, etc. (*see* eliminative MATERIALISM).

foreknowledge Knowledge of the future. It is often assumed that God has perfect foreknowledge.

formal cause *See* EFFICIENT / FORMAL / MATERIAL / FINAL CAUSES.

formal logic *See* LOGICAL FORM.

formal system A systematic and rigorous set of statements, rules, etc., whose total structure and procedures are specified — like SYMBOLIC LOGIC, but unlike ordinary language, which doesn't state (and perhaps doesn't even have) rigorous rules.

form, logical *See* LOGICAL FORM.

forms, Platonic *See* PLATONIC FORMS.

formula Any series of symbols in SYMBOLIC LOGIC. *See also* WELL-FORMED FORMULA.

formula, well-formed *See* WELL-FORMED FORMULA.

Foucault, Michel (1926-1984) French philosopher, historian, author, associated with the STRUCTURALISTS. Best known for his works attempting to uncover the underlying structure and PRESUPPOSITIONS of the ideas of madness and sexuality in Western civilization.

foundationalism The position that there is a particular sort of statement (sometimes thought to be INDUBITABLE) from which all other statements comprising a system of belief should be derived. There are foundationalist theories of knowledge, of ethics, etc.

four causes *See* EFFICIENT / FORMAL / MATERIAL / FINAL CAUSES.

freedom 1. Personal freedom (*see* FREE WILL). **2.** Political freedom is what people have insofar as they are unrestricted by laws, or insofar as they have RIGHTS. What constitutes political freedom, and to what extent it is a good thing, is a central concern of political philosophy. **3.** A variable is free when it is unbound (*see* SYMBOLS OF QUANTIFIED LOGIC).

free will Free will (or FREEDOM 1) is the supposed human characteristic that our decisions and actions are sometimes entirely (or at least partially) "up to us" — not forced or DETERMINED by anything internal or external to us. We can then either do or not do x — we have alternatives. It seems that only if we have free will can we be RESPONSIBLE for what we do. But if determinism is true, then everything must be the way it is given its previous CAUSES, including all our actions and decisions; because these causes are themselves determined by still earlier causes, ultimately whatever we decide or do is determined by events that happened a long time ago, and that are not up to us. Thus, it seems that determinism is incompatible with free will. There are three main responses to this apparent problem: (1) Hard determinists accept determinism, so deny free will. (2) LIBERTARIANS accept free will, so deny determinism, at least for some human events (*see* CONTRA-CAUSAL FREEDOM) Both libertarianism and hard determinism are incompatiblist (*see* COMPATIBLISM); that is, they hold that the freedom of an act is incompatible with its being determined. (3) Soft Determinists are compatiblists, in that they attack the reasoning above, and argue that our actions might be determined, but also free in some sense — that a determined action might nevertheless be up to the doer, and one that the doer is morally responsible for — when it's determined but not compelled (*see* COMPULSION).

Frege, Gottlob (1848-1925) German logician and philosopher of language, the founder of modern mathematical logic. He is best known for inventing quantification in logic (*see* SYMBOLS OF QUANTIFIER LOGIC), for his arguments that mathematics should be understood as an extension of logic, and for his investigations into the relation between sense and reference (*see* DENOTATION / CONNOTATION) in philosophy of language. ['FRAY-guh']

frequency theory of probability *See* PROBABILITY.

Freud, Sigmund *See* SCIENTISTS.

function 1. Loosely speaking, a correspondence between one group of things and another. The notion has its home in arithmetic, where, for example, y is said to be a function of x in the FORMULA $y = x^2$. Thus, each value of x corresponds to a value of y: if x is 1 then y is 1, if x is 2 then y is 4, and so on. The value you stick in (in place of x, in this case) is called the 'argument' of the function, and what you get out (the corresponding value of y, in this case) is called the 'value' of the function for that argument. Given the argument 3, the value is 9. *See*, also, TRUTH-FUNCTIONALITY. **2.** The function of something is its use, goal, proper or characteristic activity, the way it normally fits into CAUSAL relations with other things (*see* FUNCTIONALISM, FUNCTIONAL KIND).

functionalism The view that a certain sort of thing is actually a FUNCTIONAL KIND. A widely discussed view is functionalism about mental states: that each sort of mental state is a functional kind, definable in terms of its typical causes and effects. Functionalists tend to be token (*see* TYPE / TOKEN) MATERIALISTS, because they think that a particular internal state described functionally would be a particular physical state of the person's brain, though each type of mental state need not correspond to a type of physical state (*see*, by analogy, the can-opener example, in FUNCTIONAL KIND).

functional kind A functional kind is a categorization in terms of what things can do – what their cause-and-effect relations with the world are – and not in terms of what they are made of, or how they are constructed. 'Can opener', for example, names a functional kind, because a can opener is anything whose operations result in a can being opened; this kind admits a wide variety of different physical kinds of things (compare an old-fashioned lever-tool, the can opener you turn, the electric can opener). (*See also* DEFINITION).

function, truth *See* TRUTH-FUNCTION.

future contingents, problem of *See* PROBLEM OF FUTURE CONTINGENTS.

G

Galileo, Galilei *See* SCIENTISTS.

gambler's fallacy You might think (as many people, not only gamblers, do) that the fact that a fair coin has been flipped five times and has come up heads every time means it's much more likely to come up tails the next (to "try" to even out the frequency). If you do, you're wrong. If it's really a fair coin, the PROBABILITY that it will come up tails is .5 for the sixth flip, as it is for each flip. (Also called the 'Monte Carlo fallacy'.)

game theory A systematic mathematical theory of human interaction that sees it as a rule-governed, sometimes competitive, group activity with certain aims and strategies. Most centrally a theory of economic behaviour, but also applied to other sorts of human interactions, such as political and moral ones.

general idea *See* CONCEPT.

generalization A statement or judgement that ABSTRACTS or reasons from particular cases to a more broadly or universally applicable statement or judgment, or the process of doing this. Generalization occurs in inductive logic (*see* DEDUCTION / INDUCTION when we reason from characteristics of one or a few individuals to a statement about all individuals of that type; in deductive logic when we derive a quantified (*see* QUANTIFIER LOGIC) statement; and in ethics when we think about rules that everyone should follow.

general will What is desired by, or desirable for, society as a whole; sometimes taken to be the appropriate JUSTIFICATION for government policy. This notion has seemed to many quite mysterious when it is taken (in its classical formulation by ROUSSEAU, for instance) to mean something other than what's revealed by majority vote or unanimity.

Genetic fallacy The mistaken argument that the origins of something are the thing itself, or that its origins prove something about it. One form of this is the AD HOMINEM argument.

genius, evil *See* EVIL GENIUS.

genus / species For philosophers, not just biological hierarchical divisions, but divisions anywhere. A genus is a general classification; a species subdivides the genus. This nomenclature is especially associated with ARISTOTLE, who thought that a species ought to be defined by giving the ESSENTIAL characteristics of its genus, plus the differentia (Latin: "differences") that distinguish that species from others in the genus. For an argument against the universal applicability of this sort of definition, *see* FAMILY RESEMBLANCE.

ghost in the machine RYLE's disparaging term for how mind / body DUALISTS see persons: as a physical, mechanical body containing a ghostly, non-material mind. He argued that minds are, like ghosts, thought to exist because of philosophically mistaken reasoning. (*see* CATEGORY MISTAKE).

given The given is the sort of thing that is the ground floor of our knowledge: that for which there is no evidence, but which counts as evidence for anything else. For example, perception is often supposed to provide the given. Some philosophers doubt that there is anything that is given in this sense. (*See also* DATUM, FOUNDATIONALISM).

gnosticism The doctrine of the Gnostics, an early marginally Christian sect, who offered salvation through otherwise hidden knowledge of spiritual truths (rather than through faith), and advocated transcending the material world. ['NOS-ti-sizm')

God Among traditional Christians and Jews, God is the supernatural creator of the universe, who provides the source for morality, answers our prayers, is all-powerful and all-knowing, cares for us, and provides for immortality and salvation. With a lower-case 'g', 'god' refers to any other supernatural being believed in by other religions. There has been frequent philosophical debate about whether God's existence can be proven rationally. For a list of many classical attempts to do this, *see* ARGUMENTS FOR GOD'S EXISTENCE.

Gödel, Kurt (1906-1977) Austrian-born American mathematician and LOGICIAN, widely known for Gödel's theorem: his proof of the INCOMPLETENESS of any CONSISTENT logic strong enough to include elementary number theory. [The closest many English-speakers can get to pronouncing his name is 'girdle' — that's closer than 'go-del', anyway]

golden mean *See* MEAN.

Golden Rule A principle of morality associated with Christianity: "Do unto others as you would have them do unto you."

good, intrinsic / extrinsic / instrumental *See* INTRINSIC / EXTRINSIC / INSTRUMENTAL GOOD.

good faith *See* BAD FAITH / GOOD FAITH / AUTHENTICITY / INAUTHENTICITY.

Goodman, (Henry) Nelson (b. 1906) Contemporary American philosopher associated (together with QUINE) with contemporary PRAGMATISM; influential writings in theory of knowledge, philosophy of language and of science, and METAPHYSICS.

good / right Both terms of moral approval. The distinction between them isn't very strict, but sometimes 'good' is taken to apply to people or things, and 'right' to actions. (*see also* ACT / AGENT MORALITIES).

grammar Philosophers use this word in a wider way than English teachers do. It means the form, that is, the general structure, of a sentence. This can include its LOGICAL FORM as well as its SYNTAX. Linguists sometimes include in grammar the SEMANTICS and PHONETICS of a sentence as well. For the distinction between depth and surface grammar, *see* DEEP / SURFACE STRUCTURE.

greatest happiness principle *See* UTILITARIANISM.

Greek Academy —*see* ACADEMY.

Grelling's paradox Named for the German logician Kurt Grelling. Some adjectives apply to themselves, for example, 'English', 'short', 'polysyllabic'. Call these 'autological' adjectives. Some adjectives do not apply to themselves, for example, 'French', 'long', 'monosyllabic'. Call these 'heterological' adjectives. Now consider the adjective 'heterological'. Is this a heterological adjective? This, like the LIAR'S PARADOX, is a paradox of SELF-REFERENCE.

Grice, H(erbert) P(aul) (1913-1988) English philosopher with influential work on METAPHYSICS and EPISTEMOLOGY.

grue A colour name invented by Nelson GOODMAN, defined as follows:

x is grue if and only if:

(1) It is before time t and x is green; or

(2) It is t or after and x is blue.

Let t be some future time, say midnight tonight. All emeralds observed so far have been green, so they have also been grue. Using the usual inductive reasoning process (*see* DEDUCTION / INDUCTION), you conclude that they will be green tomorrow. But all those emeralds have also been grue; the same reasoning shows that they will be grue tomorrow; but that means they will be blue tomorrow. Both predictions can't be correct; why do you think only the first is? Goodman raised what he called the "new riddle of induction" (*see* PROBLEM OF INDUCTION for the "old riddle"): we all think that green is a PROJECTIBLE property and grue isn't, but Goodman argued there's no JUSTIFICATION for this.

H

Habermas, Jürgen (b. 1929) German social philosopher, widely known for his rejection of POSITIVISM and EMPIRICISM in favour of an ANALYSIS of knowledge in terms of social theory.

haecceity This penny looks a lot like any other penny, and some other pennies look exactly alike. Is there some characteristic that only this penny has, and only this one could have—for example, the characteristic of *being* this penny? This is a peculiar sort of characteristic, but some MEDIEVAL and contemporary philosophers argue that it's necessary to distinguish any particular thing from every other actual and possible thing. This sort of characteristic is called in Latin a 'haecceitas' (a "this-ness"), in English a 'haecceity'. The belief that such characteristics exist is haecceitism. ['hex-EYE-ih-tee' or 'hex-AY-ih-tee'; 'HEX-ee-a-tizm']

hallucination *See* ILLUSION / HALLUCINATION / DELUSION.

happiness Some philosophers, especially those who believe that happiness is one, or the only, basic element in a good life, think of happiness not as merely feeling jolly, but in a more complex way; for example, as characterizing a life that achieves whatever they consider to be its highest goal.

happiness calculus *See* FELICIFIC CALCULUS.

hard determinism *See* FREE WILL.

Hare, R(ichard) M. (b. 1919) Contemporary British philosopher, best known for his views on ethics.

hedonism In ordinary talk, this is seeking or desiring what some call the "lower" pleasures—wine, persons of the opposite sex, and song. In philosophical talk, this term also has to do with pleasure. Philosophical hedonists, however, often distinguish between the "higher" and "lower" pleasures, making the former more important. As in the case of EGOISM, we may distinguish psychological hedonism, the claim that people in fact seek only pleasure, from ethical hedonism, the claim that people ought to seek pleasure (or only pleasure). The philosophical hedonists include EPICURUS, LOCKE, HOBBES, HUME, BENTHAM, and MILL. ['HEE-dun-izm'. 'Hedonic' means 'pertaining to pleasure'; pronounced 'heh-DON-ik' or 'hee-DON-ik']

hedonic calculus *See* FELICIFIC CALCULUS.

Hegel, Georg Wilhelm Friedrich (1770-1831) Foremost of the German IDEALISTS, still an enormous influence on CONTINENTAL philosophy; at the end of the nineteenth century, most English-speaking philosophers were Hegelians. Known for his "DIALECTICAL" philosophy of history, of thought, and of the universe as a whole, which is seen as the progressive unfolding of reason—of the "Absolute Idea". ['HAY-gul')

Heidegger, Martin (1899-1976) German founder of EXISTENTIALIST PHENOMENOLOGY. He attempted to provide a theory of the "authentic self" based on the feeling of dread and the awareness of death. ['HIGH-digger']

Heisenberg, Werner *See* SCIENTISTS.

Heisenberg Uncertainty Principle *See* UNCERTAINTY PRINCIPLE.

Helmholtz, Herman Ludwig von *See* SCIENTISTS.

Hempel, Carl (Gustav) (b. 1905) German-born American philosopher, member of the VIENNA CIRCLE, important in philosophy of science and contemporary EMPIRICISM. ['HEM-pl']

Heraclitus of Ephesus (5th century B.C.) PRE-SOCRATIC philosopher who taught that all things were composed of fire, and in constant flux. ['hair-uh-KLY-tus']

heresy An opinion rejected as contrary to the official doctrine of a religious group, and officially prohibited by that religion.

hermeneutics The practice of interpretation or EX-PLANATION; once closely associated with interpretation of the Bible, but now used (especially in CONTINENTAL circles) to mean a general science or methodology of interpretation. [English speakers usually say 'her-man-OO-ticks' or 'her-man-YOU-ticks']

heterodox *See* ORTHODOX / HETERODOX.

heterogeneous *See* HOMOGENEOUS / HETEROGENEOUS.

heterological *See* SELF-REFERENCE.

heteronomy *See* AUTONOMY / HETERONOMY.

historical materialism / idealism Philosophers of history sometimes argue about what sorts of things are the most basic items at work in the process of history. We ordinarily think that these factors are people, economic conditions, countries, etc., but some philosophers have speculated that there is some sort of invisible "idea" or "spirit" whose operations underlie, at the most basic level, the most general historical processes. These philosophers are called 'historical idealists'. Those who insist that history gets its structure from merely physical things and processes are the historical materialists; this view is especially strongly associated with MARX. *See also* DIALECTICAL MATERIALISM / IDEALISM.

historicism 1. A view that emphasizes the variability of belief among historical periods; thus it tends to RELATIVISM. **2.** The view that certain human phenomena cannot be understood in isolation from their historical development and from their significance to the particular historical period in which they existed, and to the people in this period.

Hobbes, Thomas (1588-1679) English philosopher, a crucial figure associated with the birth of MODERN PHILOSOPHY. Hobbes was instrumental in replacing the earlier ARISTOTELIAN view of change as motion from potentiality to actuality with a modern MATERIALISTIC, MECHANISTIC view: atoms in motion, interacting because of their physical properties, not purposes, explain the world. Hobbes is also associated with the view that strong government is justified by a SOCIAL CONTRACT in which naturally selfish citizens bind themselves for their mutual protection and well-being. ['hobz']

holism / individualism It is sometimes held that certain sorts of things, events, or processes are more than merely the sum of their parts—that they can be understood only by examining them as a whole. This position is called 'holism' (rarely spelled 'wholism'), sometimes contrasted with 'individualism'. In social science and history, for example, holists argue that one can't explain

what's going on on the basis of individual people's AC-
TIONS, because these get their significance only by virtue
of facts about the whole society. Voting, for example, is
not just the sum of the individual actions of marking on a
piece of paper or pushing down a lever: its significance
can be explained only by thinking about it *as* voting—
that is, by appealing to characteristics applying only to
the society as a whole. Holism about meaning (associated with QUINE) insists that words and sentences
get their meaning only through their relationships with
all other words and sentences. Holism about living
things refuses to see them merely as the sum of their
non-living parts. *See also* EMERGENT PROPERTIES,
REDUCTIONISM, VITALISM.

homogeneous / heterogeneous Something   that's
homogeneous is the same throughout; heterogeneous
collections contain different sorts of things. ['het-er-oh'
or 'ho-mo' + '-JE-nee-us']

homological *See* SELF-REFERENCE.

honorific An honorific term is one that carries, as part of
its meaning, an IMPLICATION of praise. To call someone
'brave', for example, is not just to say that that person is
steadfast in the presence of danger—it's also to praise
that person. 'Brave' and 'rash' are applied to someone
depending entirely on whether you want to praise or dis-
parage that person's steadfastness in the face of danger.
If you refuse to call someone who runs from battlefield
danger a 'soldier', you are using that word as an
honorific, in a way not central to its basic sense in
English: some soldiers are faint-hearted. *See also*
DEFINITION 7.

horns of a dilemma *See* DILEMMA.

horseshoe A SYMBOL OF SENTENTIAL LOGIC, '⊃', used to form a material CONDITIONAL. 'P ⊃ Q' is roughly equivalent to 'If P then Q'.

humanism Any view that centres on the value and dignity of humans, or that makes actual human values and relevance for humans the central starting points. Associated with the Renaissance movement, which turned away from medieval supernaturalism and other-worldliness and emphasized human worth and FREEDOM 2. 'LIBERAL' (or 'secular') humanist has come to characterize of anyone who de-emphasizes religion and advocates LIBERTY 2, tolerance, and human welfare seen in terms of "earthly" values. It's sometimes a derogatory term, when used by right-wing believers to characterize left-wing ATHEISTS or anything thought to be consistent with their views.

Hume, David (1711-1776) Scottish philosopher and historian, among the greatest philosophers of all time. A thoroughgoing EMPIRICIST, he believed that all our ideas were copies of sense impressions (*see* IDEA / IMPRESSION); he argued that many of our notions (such as the continuing "self," and the necessary connection we suppose exists between CAUSE and effect, since unsupported by perception, are mistaken, and that A PRIORI knowledge must derive merely from logical relations between ideas. He is famous also for SCEPTICAL conclusions regarding moral "knowledge": our ethical reactions, he argued, come merely from the psychological tendency to feel SYMPATHY with others. His scepticism and empiricism were enormously influential in the ANALYTIC PHILOSOPHICAL tradition, and make him seem quite contemporary to us.

Husserl, Edmund (1859-1938) German-Czech philosopher and mathematician, founder of PHENOMENOLOGY; influenced by BRENTANO, and greatly influential on EXISTENTIALISM. His method involved "BRACKETING" experience—considering limited aspects of it so that the ESSENCES of things are revealed.

Hutcheson, Francis (1694-?1746) Irish-born philosopher who worked in Ireland and Scotland; known for the theory of the "moral sense," a kind of perception whereby feelings of approval or disapproval are raised in us.

Huxley, Thomas *See* SCIENTISTS.

hypostatization *See* REIFICATION.

hypothesis A tentative suggestion that may be merely a guess or a hunch, or may be based on some sort of reasoning; in any case it needs further evidence to be rationally acceptable as true. Some philosophers think that all scientific enquiry begins with hypotheses. [*Note*: singular 'hypothesis'; plural 'hypotheses']

hypothetical entities *See* THEORETICAL ENTITIES.

hypothetical imperative *See* CATEGORICAL / HYPOTHETICAL IMPERATIVE.

hypothetical syllogism A form of valid deductive reasoning (*see* ARGUMENT):
    If p then q.
    If q then r.
    Therefore, if p then r.

hypothetico-deductive model The view of the structure of science that sees it as the process in which first a

HYPOTHESIS is formed; then statements about particular, observable facts are DERIVED from this hypothesis; and then the hypothesis is confirmed by CONFIRMATION of these statements.

I

idea In general, any thought or perception in the mind. Sometimes used to refer to a PLATONIC FORM. HUME used this word in a special way (*see* IDEA / IMPRESSION).

idea, general / abstract *See* CONCEPT.

idea / impression In HUME, an impression is the mental event (= SENSE-DATUM) one has as the immediate result of, and while, using one's senses. Impressions leave their imprint on the mind, and ideas, the fainter copy of these impressions, may be called up later in the absence of sensation.

idealism In the ordinary sense of the word, an idealist is one who adheres to moral principle, or who is an impractical dreamer. This has little to do with its philosophical sense. Philosophically, METAPHYSICAL idealism is the view that only minds and their contents really or basically exist—a form of monism (*see* DUALISM / MONISM / PLURALISM); and EPISTEMOLOGICAL idealism is the view that the only things we know (or know directly) are our own IDEAS.

idealism, historical *See* HISTORICAL MATERIALISM / IDEALISM.

ideal language An artificial language (*see* ARTIFICIAL / NATURAL LANGUAGE) constructed in such a way that it contains all the ASSERTIONS we'd want to make in a certain area, in unambiguous and simplest form, and only assertions; and so that the logical relations between these assertions are clear and unambiguous. Natural languages are clearly not ideal languages. Some philosophers think that the construction of an ideal language is an important step in producing a THEORY. An aim of SYMBOLIC LOGIC is to produce an ideal language.

ideal observer theory A theory of ethics that attempts to explain what is really good by relying on the ethical reactions of an ideal observer — that is, someone who would have all the relevant information, and who would not be misled by particular INTERESTS or biases.

ideas, abstract *See* CONCEPT.

ideas, clear and distinct *See* CLEAR AND DISTINCT IDEAS.

ideas, innate *See* INNATENESS.

ideas, Platonic *See* PLATONIC FORMS.

ideas, simple / complex *See* SIMPLE / COMPLEX IDEAS.

identity 1. Your identity is what you are — what's important about you, or what makes you different from everyone else. **2.** x and y are said to be identical when x and y are in fact the same thing — when 'x' and 'y' are two different names or ways of REFERRING to exactly the same object. This differs somewhat from the ordinary way of talking, in which two different things might be said to be 'identical' when they are exactly alike in some characteristics. Sometimes philosophers call this second kind of identity 'qualitative identity' — i.e., identity of qualities or characteristics; and the first sort of identity 'quantitative identity'. (Quantitative) identity is thus the logical relation that holds between a and b, when a and b are actually the same thing. This is symbolised using the equals sign: a = b (*see* SYMBOLS OF QUANTIFIER LOGIC). **3.** Identity (over time) is the relation between something at one time and that same thing at another time: they are said to be two 'temporal stages' of the same continuing thing. Note that two stages of the same thing are not quantitatively identical (they're different stages), and need not even be qualitatively identical: you're now taller than when you were an infant. *See also* PROBLEM OF IDENTITY, PERSONAL IDENTITY, BALL OF WAX.

identity of indiscernibles *See* LAW OF THE IDENTITY OF INDISCERNIBLES.

identity, law of *See* LAWS OF THOUGHT.

identity, personal *See* PERSONAL IDENTITY.

identity theory of mind The view that each mental state is really a physical state, probably of the brain. Often identity theorists believe in addition in the TYPE-identity of mental and physical states (*see* IDENTITY 2).

ideology A system of values and beliefs, especially one concerning social and political matters. MARX thought of official ideological systems as delusions resulting from the false consciousness of the class societies in which they developed. Even in the mouths of non-Marxists, the word 'ideology' may suggest official mass illusion. ['eye-' or 'ih-' + '-dee-OL-o-jee']

idiolect A language or variant on a language used by only one person. ['ID-ee-o-lect']

if and only if *See* BICONDITIONAL.

iff An abbreviation for 'if and only if'. *See* BICONDITIONAL.

ignoratio elenchi (Latin: "by ignoring the issues") The sort of reasoning that is faulty because the premises are irrelevant to the conclusion, or, more narrowly, when a well-known and obvious ARGUMENT to the contrary is ignored. ['ig-no' + '-RAHT-' or '-RAHTZ' + '-ee-o eh-LENK-ee']

illocutionary / perlocutionary act / intention Distinctions associated with John SEARLE and J. L. AUSTIN. Illocutionary and perlocutionary INTENTIONS 1 are intentions of special sorts that we have when using language in communication. An illocutionary act is one that is accomplished merely by the hearer's (or reader's) understanding what we're doing: thus, illocutionary acts include *informing* somebody of something, *asking* somebody about something, *ordering* somebody to do something, and so on. Of course, often we have further intentions regarding the hearer: when I say 'Please close the door' I intend not only to perform the illocutionary act of requesting that you close the door, but also to perform the further act of getting you to close the door because of this request. This further act is a perlocutionary act: getting you to respond in some way because of my illocutionary act and your recognition of it. My intentions to perform illocutionary and perlocutionary acts are called illocutionary and perlocutionary intentions. Austin, Searle, and others argue that a good way to explain the meanings of parts of a language is to specify how the rules of the language create the potential for each bit to perform illocutionary acts.

illusion / hallucination / delusion 1. Illusions and hallucinations are "false" perceptual experiences—ones that lead, or could lead, to mistakes about what is out there. A hallucination is the apparent perception of something that does not exist at all (as in dreaming, mirages, drug-induced states). An illusion is the incorrect perception of something that does exist (examples are the MÜLLER-LYER ILLUSION, and the familiar way a straight stick half-immersed in water looks bent). A delusion is a perception that actually results in a false belief; illusions and hallucinations can delude, but often do not. The ARGUMENT FROM ILLUSION draws EPISTEMOLOGICAL conclusions from the existence of these things. **2.** 'Illusion' and 'delusion' are sometimes used to refer to any false belief: Freud (*see* SCIENTISTS) and MARX called religious beliefs "illusions."

imagination In the ordinary sense, this is our faculty for thinking things up, especially unreal things. Some philosophers have used this word to refer to the faculty of having images — mental pictures.

immanent *See* TRANSCENDENT / IMMANENT.

immaterialism The view that some things exist that are not material: that are not made of ordinary physical stuff, but instead of mental or spiritual — immaterial (synonym: 'incorporeal') — stuff. This is the denial of MATERIALISM. The most extreme form of immaterialism is the view that no material things exist: this is IDEALISM.

immaterial substance *See* SUBSTANCE.

immediate 1. In the ordinary sense, this means 'without delay' but **2.** in its more technical philosophical sense it means 'without mediation' — that is, 'directly'. In this sense, for example, philosophers ask whether external things are sensed immediately, or mediated by the sensing of internal images.

immorality / amorality The first means 'contrary to morality'; the second, 'without morality'. Someone who knows about moral rules but intentionally disobeys them or rejects them is immoral; someone who doesn't know or think about morality is amoral.

immortality The supposed continuation of the soul or spirit or mind or person forever, after the death of the body. It is, of course, a central feature of the beliefs of most religions, but philosophers have sometimes argued against the possibility (and even the desirability) of immortality.

imperative A statement telling you what to do.

imperative, categorical / hypothetical *See* CATEGORICAL / HYPOTHETICAL IMPERATIVE.

implication / inference A logical relation that holds between two statements when the second follows DEDUCTIVELY from the first. The first is then said to 'imply' the second; this relation is sometimes called 'implication'. Be careful not to confuse 'implication' with 'inference': the first is a relation between statements, but the second is something people do, when they reason from one statement to another (which the first statement implies). A rule of inference is an acceptable procedure for reasoning from one set of statements of a particular form to another statement. For a different sort of use, *see* 'material implication' and 'strict implication', in CONDITIONAL.

implicature *See* IMPLICATION / INFERENCE.

imply / infer *See* IMPLICATION / INFERENCE.

import, existential *See* EXISTENTIAL IMPORT.

impression *See* IDEA / IMPRESSION.

inalienable right *See* RIGHTS.

inauthenticity *See* BAD FAITH / GOOD FAITH / AUTHEN-TICITY / INAUTHENTICITY.

inclination Any desire, or pro or con feeling. Some philosophers (KANT is a good example) think that acting from inclination cannot be moral action; the only right actions are those motivated by an understanding of duty, and are often contrary to inclination.

inclusive or / disjunction *See* DISJUNCTION.

incoherent *See* COHERENT.

incompatiblism *See* FREE WILL.

incompleteness *See* COMPLETENESS / INCOMPLETENESS.

inconsistency *See* CONSISTENCY.

incorrigibility / corrigibility Something is incorrigible when it is impossible to correct it, or when it is guaranteed correct. 'Corrigibility' means 'correctibility'. Some philosophers have thought that our beliefs about our own mental states are incorrigible. For example, if you sincerely believe that you are now feeling a pain, how could you be wrong?

incorporeality *See* IMMATERIALITY.

indefinite description *See* DEFINITE / INDEFINITE DESCRIPTION.

indeterminacy of translation The view, associated most closely with QUINE, that there are many possible ways to translate another language into your own, and that there may not be conclusive reasons to prefer one translation to another. Quine argued that there is no fact of the matter about what someone means by what he / she says; there is only a preferred translation. *See also* RADICAL TRANSLATION.

indeterminacy, principle of *See* PRINCIPLE OF INDETERMINACY.

indeterminism *See* DETERMINISM.

indexical *See* DEMONSTRATIVE / INDEXICAL.

indirect proof Proof of a statement accomplished by ASSUMING **2** its denial and deriving a SELF-CONTRADICTION or ABSURDITY from that. Also known as *reductio ad absurdum* (Latin: "reduction to the absurd").

indiscernibles *See* LAW OF THE IDENTITY OF INDISCERNIBLES.

individual constant *See* VARIABLE / CONSTANT.

individual essence *See* ESSENCE.

individual / individuation 1. In ordinary talk, the word 'individual' can be used correctly as a contrast to 'group', 'organization', etc., but is frequently misused as a pompous synonym for 'person'. **2.** In philosophical talk, an individual is a single thing (not necessarily a person) that is basic in the sense of not being ANALYZABLE into parts. Individuation is distinguishing between one thing and another: philosophers sometimes try to discover criteria for individuation of some sort of thing, that is, the tests we use to tell things of that sort from one another, and to count how many of them there are in a group of them. 'Particulars' is a synonym for 'individuals'.

individual variable *See* VARIABLE / CONSTANT.

individuation *See* INDIVIDUAL / INDIVIDUATION.

indubitability / dubitability 'Dubitable' means 'doubtable'. Dubitable statements are not just ones we are psychologically capable of doubting, but ones about which even highly fanciful and unlikely doubts might be raised, doubts that no one in his / her right mind would seriously have. Thus DESCARTES thought that because our senses might be fooled, information from them was dubitable. He then went on to try to discover what sort of belief was really indubitable: about which it could be proven that no doubt can be raised. *See also* CERTAIN.

induction *See* DEDUCTION / INDUCTION.

induction, problem of *See* PROBLEM OF INDUCTION.

ineffable Indescribable, not communicable. Some religious or mystical experiences are said to be ineffable.

inference *See* IMPLICATION / INFERENCE.

infinite regress A sequence that must continue backwards endlessly. For example, if every event must have a cause, then a present event must be caused by some past event; and this event by another still earlier, and so on infinitely. Sometimes the fact that reasoning leads to an infinite regress shows that it is faulty.

informal fallacies *See* FALLACY.

informal / formal logic The latter is that kind of logic that relies heavily on SYMBOLS and rigorous procedures much like mathematics; it concentrates on reasoning that is correct because of syntax. (*see* SEMANTICS / SYNTAX / PRAGMATICS). Only a small fraction of the ordinary sorts of reasoning we do can be explained this way, and there is a vast scope for informal logic, which analyzes good and bad arguments semantically, and relies less heavily on symbols and mathematics-style procedures.

inherent *See* INTRINSIC / INHERENT / INSTRUMENTAL / EXTRINSIC.

in-itself / for-itself These are the two fundamental categories SARTRE thought the world was divided into. The realm of the for-itself (in French, '*pour-soi*', ['poor swa']) includes free things—things that are conscious, create their own characteristics, and are RESPONSIBLE for everything they do. This realm is often though to include only PERSONS. The realm of the in-itself (French: 'en-soi', [roughly, 'ah-swa']) includes everything else. (For a different sense of 'in-itself', *see* THING-IN-ITSELF.)

innateness A belief, CONCEPT, or characteristic is innate when it is inborn—when it doesn't come from experience or education—though experience may be thought necessary to make conscious or actualize something that is given innately. An argument for the innateness of something is that experience is not sufficient to produce it in us. Well-known innateness views are PLATO's (for the innateness of concepts) and CHOMSKY's (for the innateness of concepts and of the basic structures of language).

innocence and guilt The DETERRENCE theory of PUNISHMENT claims that inflicting punishment is JUSTIFIED if this prevents future undesirable acts. But suppose that punishing someone who was in fact innocent prevented a great deal of future crime (by others); it seems that this would be justified by the deterrence theory. Does this show that the theory is wrong? A second way innocence and guilt enter into a philosophical argument is in the theory of the "just war." Many people are willing to allow that going to war under some circumstances is morally justified; but in every war innocent people are hurt and killed. Does this show that it's acceptable to harm innocent people? Or that there's something wrong with "just war" theory?

in principle Contrasted with 'in fact' or 'in practice'. Philosophers talk about things we can do in principle, meaning that we could do them if we had the time or technology, or if other merely practical difficulties did not stand in the way. For example, we can VERIFY the statement 'There is a red pebble lying on the north pole of Mars' in principle, though at the moment we can't test this by observation. We might forever be unable to test statements about extremely distant stars, but these are verifiable in principle. In principle, one can count to one quadrillion, because we know the rules for doing it, though in fact we lack the patience and wouldn't live long enough anyway.

instrumental *See* INTRINSIC / INHERENT / INSTRUMENTAL / EXTRINSIC.

instrumentalism *See* OPERATIONALISM / INSTRUMENTALISM.

intelligence, artificial *See* ARTIFICIAL INTELLIGENCE.

intelligibility / unintelligibility Something is intelligible when it is possible to understand it; otherwise, unintelligible.

intensional *See* EXTENSION / INTENSION.

intentional Note the second 't' in this word; be careful not to confuse it with 'intensional' (*see* EXTENSION / INTENSION). **1.** Sometimes 'intentional' means 'on purpose', or 'having to do with intentions' (i.e., plans or desires about ACTIONS). **2.** Intentionality is the idea that mental events have objects which they "intend" or point to; thus, thinking that Bolivia is in South America has as intentional objects—is about—Bolivia and South America. Some thoughts have *merely* intentional, not real, objects, however: thinking about Santa Claus is not thinking about a real object because (bad news!) there is no Santa. Intentional objects are sometimes called 'subsistent ENTITIES', by contrast to 'existent entities'.

interactionism A form of mind / body DUALISM. It holds that mind and body can interact—that is, that mental events can cause physical events (e.g., when your decision to touch something causes your physical hand movement) and that physical events can cause mental events (e.g., when a physical stimulation to your body causes a mental feeling of pain). A standard objection to this commonsense position is that it's hard to see how this sort of causal interaction could take place, since the mental and the physical work according to their own laws: how could an electrical impulse in a (physical) nerve cell cause a non-physical pain in a mind? Perhaps this even violates the law of conservation of energy. DESCARTES was a classical interactionist.

interests Not, as in an ordinary sense, those things about which you are curious or fascinated; rather, that which is of value to you. Something may be thought to a (real) interest of yours even though you don't think you want it—it's an objective, not a subjective, interest. Sometimes interests are distinguished from needs: you can't do without the latter. Thus food is a need, but watching TV is only an interest.

interpretation, radical *See* RADICAL TRANSLATION / INTERPRETATION.

interpreted calculus *See* CALCULUS.

intersection / union of sets The intersection of two SETS (also known as the 'product' of the two) is the set of things these two sets hold in common; the union (also known as the 'sum' of the two) is the set of things including both of them. Thus the intersection of the set of dogs and the set of brown things is the set of brown dogs; the intersection of the set of dogs and the set of cats is empty (i.e., there is no thing that is both a dog and a cat); the union of the set of dogs and the set of cats is the set of dogs and cats (that group of things consisting of all dogs plus all cats).

intransitive *See* TRANSITIVE / INTRANSITIVE / NONTRANSITIVE.

intrinsic / inherent / instrumental / extrinsic Some-thing valued as an intrinsic (synonym, 'inherent') good is valued just in itself, apart from its consequences; for example, one might value playing tennis just because it's enjoyable in itself. Or it might be valued as an extrinsic (synonym, 'instrumental') good: for the sake of what it results in, for example, physical fitness. An intrinsic good is sometimes called an end in itself. The distinction here is the one we refer to when we talk about valuing something as an end or as a means (*see* ENDS / MEANS). These are also kinds of RIGHTS: an intrinsic or inherent right is one people have permanently or essentially, by their very nature; the contrast here is with extrinsic rights, which they have temporarily, or have to be granted. *See also* RELATIONAL / INTRINSIC PROPERTIES.

intrinsic properties *See* RELATIONAL / INTRINSIC PROPERTIES.

introspection The capacity for finding things out about oneself by "looking inward" — by direct awareness of one's own mental states. You might find out that you have a headache, for example, by introspection. This is contrasted with the way someone else might find this out, by observing your outward behaviour — groaning, holding your head, etc. Sometimes called 'reflection' [a chiefly British alternative spelling is 'reflexion']

intuition A belief that comes IMMEDIATELY, without reasoning, argument, or evidence. Some philosophers think that certain intuitions are the reliable, rational basis for knowledge of certain sorts. Some beliefs that arise immediately when we perceive are the basis of our knowledge of the outside world (though perceptual intuitions are not always reliable). Our ethical intuitions are sometimes taken to be the basis of, and to test, ethical theories. *See also* INTUITIONISM.

intuitionism Intuitionism is any theory that holds that IN-TUITION is a valid source of knowledge. DESCARTES, SPINOZA, and LOCKE are associated with intuitionism about certain kinds of knowledge. Ethical intuitionism is the position that ethical truths are intuited. MOORE, for example, held that there is a special sort of facility for intuiting ethical truths. Nowadays, ethical theorists mostly doubt this, but many rely on what they call ethical intuitions (i.e., ethical reactions not based on theory or reasoning) as data to CONFIRM ethical theories anyway. Intuitionism in mathematics has a rather special meaning: it holds that any sort of mathematical entity exists only if it is possible to give a CONSTRUCTIVE EXISTENCE PROOF of it.

INUS condition 'INUS' is an acronym; an INUS condition is an Insufficient but Necessary part of an Unnecessary but Sufficient condition. (*see* NECESSARY / SUFFICIENT / CONDITION) For example, lightning striking a house is an INUS condition for the house's burning down: it's a necessary part of a complex of conditions for one way (not the only way) the house might burn down. J. L. Mackie (English philosopher, 1917-1981) coined this term while proposing this complex sort of condition as part of an analysis of CAUSE. ['EYE-nus']

invalid argument *See* ARGUMENT.

invalidity *See* ARGUMENT.

inverted spectrum Suppose the visual images someone gets when seeing coloured things are "inverted" from the normal ones, so that when she sees something red, she gets a violet visual image, and when she sees something yellow, she get a blue image, and so on. She uses colour words just the way everyone else does. This supposition is part of an argument for the existence of QUALIA, and against any FUNCTIONALIST or BEHAVIOURIST theory of mind.

iota operator *See* SYMBOLS OF QUANTIFIER LOGIC.

I proposition *See* A / E / I / O PROPOSITIONS.

irrational / irrationality *See* RATIONAL / IRRATIONAL.

irreflexive *See* REFLEXIVE / IRREFLEXIVE / NON-REFLEXIVE.

is / ought problem The controversy concerning whether "is-statements" (statements that say what the facts are) can imply "ought-statements" (statements of morality that say what ought to be done). HUME is an important exponent of the view that they can't; ETHICAL NATURALISTS typically claim that they can.

J

James, William (1842-1910) American (Harvard) philosopher and psychologist, the founder of modern philosophy; brought PEIRCE's PRAGMATISM to a wide audience. A strong EMPIRICIST who argued, nevertheless, in favour of religious belief on the grounds of its good practical effect on our lives.

Jaspers, Karl (1883-1969) German EXISTENTIALIST philosopher, known for his analyses of the "authentic" and "inauthentic" self. ['YAS-purs')

jointly exhaustive *See* MUTUALLY EXCLUSIVE / JOINTLY EXHAUSTIVE.

judgment Thinking that something is the case or not the case. Sometimes this word is also used as a synonym for 'PROPOSITION' or for 'ASSERTION'. [may also be spelled 'judgement']

Jung, Carl *See* SCIENTISTS.

justice What the law requires, or what is fair or correct treatment. Distributive justice is fairness of distribution of goods and benefits in a society. There is much philosophical controversy about what the principles for justice are: for example, how should we balance the right to property with equality? John RAWLS has presented an influential contemporary theory of justice.

justice, retributive *See* RETRIBUTIVISM.

justification 1. An argument to show that some statement is true, or that some act is morally acceptable. **2.** The explanation required for each step in a DERIVATION, which tells which preceding steps and which rule of INFERENCE were used to derive that step.

Kant, Immanuel (1724-1804) German philosopher, one of the most important figures in the history of philosophy. His EPISTEMOLOGICAL concern was with the "truths of reason" (for example, that everything has a CAUSE) that HUME seemed to have shown cannot be supported by experience, and are not ANALYTIC consequences of the relations between ideas. Kant thought that such knowledge was *A PRIORI* and SYNTHETIC, and that it could be accounted for by the way that any rational mind necessarily thinks. Similarly, he argued that the basis of ethics is not EMPIRICAL or psychological (for example, it cannot be based upon our actual felt desires). Ethical knowledge can be derived merely from the *a priori* form any ethical ASSERTION must have: it must be UNIVERSALIZABLE—that is, rationally applicable to everyone. Kant argued that this is equivalent to saying that the basic ethical truth was that everyone must be thought of as an end, never merely as a means (*see also* CATEGORICAL / HYPOTHETICAL IMPERATIVE). Kant's ethical theory has become a major consideration in contemporary ethics.

karma In Hinduism and Buddhism, *karma* is the sum of the results of one's actions, and is supposed to determine one's destiny, both in this life and in future REINCARNATIONS.

katharsis *See* CATHARSIS.

Kepler, Johannes —*see* SCIENTISTS.

Keynes, John Maynard —*see* SCIENTISTS.

Kierkegaard, Søren (Aabye) (1813-1855) Danish philosopher and theologian; a Lutheran minister, though a critic of conventional religion. His views on pure choice in an ABSURD context were the origin of EXISTENTIALISM; Kierkegaard, however, concentrated on individual subjectivity and freedom in a Christian framework.

kind, natural *See* NATURAL KIND.

kings, philosopher *See* PHILOSOPHER-KINGS.

knowing how / knowing that Two sorts of knowing: one knows *how* to ride a bicycle; one knows *that* Saskatoon is in Saskatchewan.

knowledge / belief Believing and knowing something both involve thinking that it's true. One can correctly be said to know something, however, only if it's true; but one can have a false belief. There is philosophical controversy about what else is different about knowledge: Must one be JUSTIFIED in thinking what one does in order to be said to know it? Must one be connected in some way with the fact one is said to know, for example, when that fact causes one's belief?

knowledge by acquaintance / by description If you have never been to the top of Mount Everest, you know it only by description—by how others have described it, or only insofar as it's called 'the top of Mount Everest'. You have knowledge by acquaintance through actual personal experience of the thing known. This distinction is due to RUSSELL.

knowledge, pure / empirical *See* EMPIRICAL.

kosmos *See* COSMOS.

Kripke, Saul A. (b. 1940) Contemporary American philosopher known for his work on philosophy of language and of psychology, and on the POSSIBLE WORLDS analysis of necessity and possibility.

L

labour theory of value The theory of (economic) value associated with MARX, which measures the value of a commodity that is in demand by the amount of labour necessary, given current technology, for its production. [American spelling is 'labor']

Lacan, Jacques (1901-1981) French STRUCTURALIST philosopher, known for his application of structural methodology to FREUDIAN psychology and for exploring its philosophical and cultural implications.

laissez-faire (French: "let [them] do") Pertaining to an economic policy of allowing free competition, without government interference or direction. A feature of what was formerly called 'LIBERAL', now (confusingly) called 'conservative', social policy. [English-speaking philosophers usually approximate the pronunciation of this as 'less-ay fair']

Lamark, Chevalier de *See* SCIENTISTS

language-game WITTGENSTEIN used this term for language and its uses, in a broad sense, including the way our language influences the way we think and act. The emphasis here is on the similarity of a language to a game: both are rule-governed systems of behaviour, and the rules vary over times and contexts.

language, ideal *See* IDEAL LANGUAGE.

language, object / meta- *See* METALANGUAGE.

language, ordinary *See* ORDINARY LANGUAGE PHILOSOPHY.

languages, artificial / natural *See* ARTIFICIAL / NATURAL LANGUAGES.

LaPlace, Pierre *See* SCIENTISTS.

large numbers, law of *See* LAW OF LARGE NUMBERS.

law 1. A RULE or principle established and enforced by government ('civil law'), or of society. **2.** A rule of morality ('moral law'). **3.** A formulation of the general regularities of the way things work, especially in nature ('NATURAL LAW'). A law of nature may be more than merely a correct description of regularities, however (*see* NOMIC).

law, covering *See* COVERING LAW.

law, natural *See* NATURAL LAW.

law of... *See* the following entries; or under what follows 'of'; or under 'PRINCIPLE OF...'.

Law of contradiction *See* LAWS OF THOUGHT.

Law of excluded middle *See* LAWS OF THOUGHT.

law of identity *See* LAWS OF THOUGHT.

Law of large numbers Suppose you flip a fair coin four times. PROBABILITY theory tells you that you're most likely to get two heads, but you wouldn't be surprised to get three heads, or one, or four, or none. But if you flip a coin one thousand times, you'll very likely get very close to one-half heads. The law of large numbers says that it is more probable that the observed frequency will be close to the frequency predicted by theory as the number of observed events increases.

law of the identity of indiscernibles The supposed law of METAPHYSICS (associated with LEIBNIZ, thus also called 'Leibniz's law') that says that if x and y are indiscernible (share all the same properties) then x and y are IDENTICAL 2—that is, that x is y. (Two different new pennies that look exactly alike are not, in this sense, indiscernible: they differ in some characteristics not revealed by ordinary observation.) Imagine two things that are alike in *every* detail: they even occupy the same space at the same time. Why then think of them as two? Wouldn't there really be only one thing?

lawlike statements Statements which have the LOGICAL FORM of LAWS 2 whether they are true or not. Part of the philosophical study of laws is the attempt to specify the logical form of any lawlike statement.

laws, De Morgan's *See* DE MORGAN'S LAWS.

laws of thought Refers to what were traditionally taken to be the three basic principles of LOGIC, and of all rational thought, clearly true and in need of no proof. These are:

The law of identity: If anything is P (i.e., has the property P), then it is P.

The law of contradiction: A sentence and its NEGATION (i.e., its denial) cannot both be true; alternatively, nothing can be both P and not-P. Also known as the law of noncontradiction.

The law of the excluded middle: Every sentence is either true or false—there is no third possibility. This means that if a sentence is shown not to be false, then it is true. Alternatively, everything must be either P or not-P. This law is also known as the principle of law of bivalence. It is the basis for IN-DIRECT PROOF. Note that this law is not the same as the law of contradiction.

These are now only rarely called 'laws of thought' (except as a historical reference) because it is widely doubted that all three (especially the second and third) must hold of all rational thought; certainly they are not all laws of all modern systems of logic.

legal positivism / realism / scepticism Legal POSITIV-ISM is the view that laws are those rules with a "law-making" pedigree — those made by people with the authority to make laws. Thus, it holds that there is no conceptual connection between law and morality. One version of legal positivism — the command theory — holds that what makes a rule a law is that it was made by people with the power to punish infractions. Legal positivists thus recognize a set of laws that pre-exist judges' decisions, and that judges apply; but legal realists argue that judges decide the law — create it — any way they like (though they may appeal to pre-existing rules as "JUSTIFICATION.") Thus legal realism turns out to be an anti-realist account of the laws! (*see* REALISM) Legal realism is a form of legal SCEPTICISM, which holds that law does not pre-exist judicial decisions; MARXISTS and some FEMINISTS also tend to be legal sceptics.

legitimacy In general, legality or appropriateness. In political theory a ruler is legitimate when he / she has the right to rule; there are many different theories of what makes a ruler legitimate.

Leibniz, Gottfried Wilhelm (1646-1716) German scientist, mathematician, and philosopher. He and Newton (*see* SCIENTISTS) independently developed the calculus. Known for the view that all propositions are necessary (*see* NECESSARY / CONTINGENT TRUTH, in this "best of all possible worlds." ['LIBE-nits']

Leibniz's law *See* LAW OF THE IDENTITY OF INDISCERNIBLES.

lemma A sub-proof: something proved in the course of, and for the purpose of, proving something else.

Lenin, V(ladimir) I(lych) (Original surname Ulyanov) (1870-1924) Russian thinker and political leader; best-known for his establishment of the structure of the communist state; but also the author of more abstract philosophical work, where he argued against antimetaphysical POSITIVISM.

Leonardo da Vinci *See* SCIENTISTS.

Lévi-Strauss, Claude (b. 1908) French STRUCTURALIST philosopher, known for his application of structuralism to anthropology, and for drawing philosophical conclusions from this application.

Lewis, C(larence) I(rving) (1883-1964) American philosopher, best-known for his work in MODAL logic and EPISTEMOLOGY.

Lewis, David K(ellogg) (b. 1941) Contemporary American philosopher known for his work on COUNTERFACTUALS and CONVENTIONS.

liar's paradox Consider this sentence:

> The sentence in the box is false.

Is it true? If it is, then what it says — that it's not true — is correct, so it's not true. But if it's not true, then it's true. It seems that it can't be either true or false. This PARADOX arises from the SELF-REFERENCE of the statement. Logicians consider what to do with this, and what its implications are. Does it mean, for example, that some indicative sentences are neither true nor false? The name 'liar's paradox' comes from versions of this such as one in which someone says, "The statement I'm making right now is a lie."

liberalism This refers to a confusingly large family of (sometimes incompatible) positions in political theory. Traditionally, liberals valued political LIBERTY — freedom — above all, and advocated less government restriction. LOCKE's advocacy of individual RIGHTS and (limited) freedom from state constraint is a classical moderate form of liberalism in this sense. Nowadays, however, those who hold this view are more likely to be called 'conservatives'; liberals often advocate more government intervention, especially when that is thought necessary for what contemporary liberals value: for freeing people from ignorance and misery, or for solving other social problems such as poverty. Contemporary liberals also characteristically advocate DEMOCRACY, rule by all. Sometimes the word is used these days merely to designate any left-wing position (or any position left of one's own — thus possibly fairly far right.) For a contemporary use, *see* 'liberal humanism', in HUMANISM.

libertarianism 1. The position that some of our actions are free in the sense of not being caused (*see* FREE WILL and CONTRA-CAUSAL FREEDOM). **2.** The political position that political LIBERTY is the most important thing in society, so restrictive laws, taxes, welfare, state economic control, etc., should be eliminated or minimized. A more specific variety of (traditional) LIBERALISM, though nowadays this position is associated with those called 'conservatives'.

liberty 1. (Metaphysical) liberty is FREE WILL. **2.** We are said to have (political) liberty to the extent that we have RIGHTS and freedom from restrictions in a society.

linguistic analysis / philosophy *See* ANALYTIC PHILOSOPHY.

Locke, John (1632-1704) English philosopher and political theorist. None of our ideas is INNATE, he argued, so all our knowledge must come from experience. This position makes him the first of the three great British EMPIRICISTS (the others are BERKELEY and HUME). Influential also in political theory, he is known for his advocacy of (traditional) LIBERALISM and NATURAL RIGHTS.

logic Loosely speaking, logic is the process of correct reasoning, and something is logical when it makes sense. Philosophers often reserve this word for things having to do with various THEORIES of correct reasoning. TRADITIONAL LOGIC included various sorts of categorization of some types of correct and incorrect reasoning, and included study of the SYLLOGISM. Nowadays, most logical theory is done by exhibiting the types of sentences, and giving rules for what correctly may be reasoned on the basis of sentences of different types, in SYMBOLIC form (that is, with symbols taking the place of logically relevant words or connections); though INFORMAL logic is also important. For a description of the two main sorts of logic, *see* DEDUCTION / INDUCTION.

logical atomism The position, associated with RUSSELL and WITTGENSTEIN, that language might be analyzed into "atomic PROPOSITIONS," the smallest and simplest sentences, each of which corresponds to an "atomic fact," one of the simplest bits of reality.

logical behaviourism *See* BEHAVIOURISM.

Blogical equivalence *See* BICONDITIONAL.

logic, alethic *See* ALETHIC.

logical falsehood *See* LOGICAL TRUTH / FALSITY.

logical form The form of a sentence is its general structure, ignoring the particular content it has. Logical form is the structure of a sentence has because of the logical words it contains. Thus, for example, 'If it's Tuesday, then I'm late for class' and 'If Peru is in Asia, then Porky is a frog' have the same overall logical form ('if P then Q'). The sort of LOGIC that works by exhibiting, often in SYMBOLIC notation, the logical form of sentences is called 'formal logic'. 'Formal' here may also refer to logic as a FORMAL SYSTEM.

logical impossibility *See* LOGICAL TRUTH / FALSITY.

logical necessity / contingency *See* LOGICAL TRUTH / FALSITY.

logical positivism A school of philosophy, subscribed to by many English-speaking philosophers during this century. Its source was the VIENNA CIRCLE, whose best-known member was Rudolf CARNAP; its propagation in the English-speaking world is due largely to Carnap, who moved to America, and to A. J. AYER in England. Greatly impressed by the EMPIRICISM and by the success and rigour of science, the logical positivists advocated that philosophers avoid speculation about matters only science and experience could settle; if a sentence was not scientifically VERIFIABLE or a matter of LOGICAL TRUTH or CONCEPTUAL TRUTH, it was nonsense and should be discarded. Thus a central tenet of logical positivism is the VERIFIABILITY CRITERION. Ethical statements were thought not verifiable, so they didn't have any literal meaning: they were sometimes thought merely to be expressions of feelings of approval or disapproval; (*see* EMOTIVISM). Arguments against the verifiability criterion resulted in the demise of logical positivism, but its influence among English-speaking philosophers who do ANALYTIC PHILOSOPHY is still strong.

logical possibility / impossibility *See* LOGICAL TRUTH / FALSITY.

logical symbol *See*: SYMBOLS OF QUANTIFIER LOGIC, SYMBOLS OF SENTENTIAL LOGIC.

logical truth / falsity A sentence is logically true (or false) when it is true (or false) merely because of its logical structure. Examples: 'All pigs are pigs' or 'Either it's raining or it's not raining'. These should be distinguished from ANALYTIC truths / falsehoods, which are true / false merely because of the meaning of its words: for example, 'All fathers are male'. Logical truths / falsehoods are also called 'logically necessary / impossible' sentences, but these should also be distinguished from (METAPHYSICALLY) necessary truths / falsehoods (*see* NECESSARY / CONTINGENT TRUTH): those that *must* be true or false. All logical truths are necessarily true, but some philosophers think that there are necessary truths that are neither analytically nor logically true. KANT thought that 'All events have a cause' is necessarily true, but not logically true, or analytically true. 'Tautology' is sometimes used as a synonym for 'logical truth', though in ordinary talk a tautology is something that says the same thing twice. Thus, 'It's raining and it's raining' is a tautology in the ordinary sense, though not in the philosophers' sense. Sentences that are neither logically true nor logically false — that are merely true or false — are said to be logically contingent truths or falsehoods.

logic, deductive *See* DEDUCTION / INDUCTION.

logic, deontic *See* DEONTIC.

logic, dialectical *See* DIALECTIC.

logic, epistemic *See* EPISTEMIC.

logic, formal *See* INFORMAL / FORMAL LOGIC.

logic, inductive *See* DEDUCTION / INDUCTION.

logic, informal *See* INFORMAL / FORMAL LOGIC.

logicism 1. The view that all NECESSARY TRUTHS are CONCEPTUAL or ANALYTIC or LOGICAL TRUTHS. HUME may be thought of as a champion of this view; EMPIRICISTS tend to be logicists. Opposed to logicism is the view that some necessity is not a matter of the way we think or talk, but a feature of external reality. KANT argued for this position. **2.** The view that mathematics can be derived from LOGIC; associated with FREGE and RUSSELL.

logic, many-valued *See* MANY-VALUED LOGIC.

logic, modal *See* MODAL LOGIC.

logic, predicate *See* QUANTIFIER LOGIC.

logic, quantifier *See* QUANTIFIER LOGIC.

logic, quantum *See* QUANTUM LOGIC.

logic, sentential *See* SENTENTIAL LOGIC.

logic, symbolic *See* SYMBOLIC LOGIC.

logic, temporal *See* TEMPORAL

logic, truth-functional *See* SENTENTIAL LOGIC.

logos (Greek: "speech," "thought," "reason," "word," "meaning,") As you might expect, given its multiplicity of meanings in Greek, this word has been used in a great variety of ways; often it refers to the principle of rationality or law that some philosophers think is responsible for the way the universe works.

love, Platonic *See* PLATONIC LOVE.

Lucretius (full name: Titus Lucretius Carus) (96?-55 B.C.) Ancient Roman poet/philosopher, who popularized the scientific and ethical views of the ATOMISTS. ['loo-KRE-shus']

M

Mach, Ernst (1838-1916) Czech / Austrian physicist and philosopher. The father of contemporary philosophy of science, he argued for a POSITIVISTIC view of knowledge based on our sensations gathered into economical theories. ['mach', where the 'ch' is a throaty hiss as in the German *'ich'*]

Machiavelli, Niccolo (1469-1527) Italian statesman and political theorist, famous (sometimes infamous) for his political theories in which he de-emphasized the secondary place of morality in practical politics. ['mack-ee-uh-VEL-lee']

Maimonides (or Moses ben Maimon) (1135-1204) Spanish-born Jewish philosopher and theologian; codifier of the Talmud.

major / middle / minor term / premise Distinctions made in TRADITIONAL LOGIC to talk about SYLLOGISMS. The major TERM 2 is the term that is the PREDICATE 2 of the conclusion. The major premise is the premise (*see* ARGUMENT) containing the major term. The minor term is the term that is the subject of the conclusion. The minor premise is the premise containing the minor term. The middle term is the term that is in both of the premises but not in the conclusion. So, for example, in the syllogism

All pigs are sloppy eaters.

Nothing that is a sloppy eater is a friendly thing.

Therefore no pigs are friendly things.

The major term is 'friendly thing'. The minor term is 'pig'. The middle term is 'sloppy eater'. The first premise is the minor premise, and the second premise the major.

Malcolm, Norman (1911-1990) American philosopher, known for expounding and applying WITTGENSTEIN's ideas and methodology.

Malebranche, Nicolas (1638-1715) French philosopher, influenced by DESCARTES; known now mostly for his OCCASIONALISM. ['mal-uh-brahnsh']

malin genie *See* EVIL GENIUS.

Malthus, *See* SCIENTISTS.

manichaeism An influential religion of the ancient world. Its best-known feature is its view that evil is a separate and basic feature of the world, along with good, and not (as some Christians held) to be seen as merely the absence of good. ['man-uh-KEE-ism'; alternative spellings 'manicheism', 'manichaeanism' 'manicheanism']

many-valued logic It is commonly thought that each indicative sentence must be either true or false (*see* 'law of the excluded middle', in LAWS OF THOUGHT). But the possibility that a sentence might be neither true nor false, and that there might be a third possibility, or many, or an infinite number, has led to two-, three-, infinite-(etc.) valued logics ('valued' here refers to TRUTH-VALUE), which work out the laws, systems, and techniques such many-valued logics might include. Also known as 'multi-valued logic'.

Marcel, Gabriel (1889-1973) French philosopher and dramatist; a THEISTIC EXISTENTIALIST.

Marcus Aurelius (or Marcus Aurelius Antoninus) (121-180) Roman Emperor, STOIC philosopher.

Marcuse, Herbert (1898-1979) German-born American philosopher, whose blend of MARX, FREUD, and EXISTENTIALISM had a great influence on revolutionary American youth in the 1960s and 1970s.

Maritain, Jacques (1882-1973) French Catholic philosopher, influential on contemporary THOMISM.

Marx, Karl (1818-1883) German philosopher and social theorist who constructed the basis for socialist and communist IDEOLOGY (*see* SOCIALISM / COMMUNISM. He accepted HEGEL's idea of the DIALECTICAL nature of change, but rejected Hegel's IDEALISM. For Marx, it is material — economic — causes that interact, and understanding these leads to understanding the sources of past oppression and the goal to which historical progress is directed: the revolution of the working class, and the development of a classless society. Marxism is today one of the major sorts of general philosophical methodology.

master morality *See* SLAVE / MASTER MORALITY.

material *See* MATERIALISM.

material biconditional *See* EQUIVALENCE.

material cause *See* EFFICIENT / FORMAL / MATERIAL / FINAL CAUSES.

material conditional *See* CONDITIONAL.

material equivalence *See* EQUIVALENCE.

material implication *See* CONDITIONAL.

materialism The ordinary meaning of this term is the desire for consumer goods, comfort, and money, rather than for more "spiritual" goods. But as a philosophical term, it means something quite different: it is the philosophical position that all that exists is physical. LUCRETIUS and HOBBES are two of the many philosophers associated with this position. Materialists about mind sometimes argue that apparently non-physical things like the soul or mind or thoughts are actually material things (*see* IDENTITY THEORY). Central-state materialists identify mental events with physical events central in the body (i.e., in the nervous system). Some materialists, however, think that categorizing things as mental is altogether a mistake (like believing in ghosts), and that mental events do not exist and this sort of talk ought to be eliminated as science progresses. They are called 'eliminative materialists'. The terms 'materialism' and 'physicalism' are usually used as synonyms, though 'physicalism' sometimes means the position that everything is explainable by physics. For the distinction between type and token materialism, *see* TYPE / TOKEN.

materialism, dialectical *See* DIALECTICAL MATERIALISM.

materialism, historical *See* HISTORICAL MATERIALISM / IDEALISM.

material substance *See* SUBSTANCE.

matter of fact / relation of ideas HUME's distinction. A matter of fact is an EMPIRICAL claim, to be discovered *a posteriori* (*see* A PRIORI / A POSTERIORI); a relation of ideas is a CONCEPTUAL or ANALYTIC or LOGICAL TRUTH, which can be known *a priori*.

maxim In KANT, a rule for action.

maximin A rule for choice among alternatives, telling you to *max*imize the *min*imum — that is, to choose the alternative whose worst features or consequences are better than the worst features or consequences of any of the alternatives. (Also known as 'minimax': perhaps the emphasis here is *min*imizing the *max*imum harm.) It's not clear that this rule is one that ought always to be applied: we might want to choose an alternative with possible but unlikely consequences worse than consequences of all other alternatives. Other rules talked about in decision theory are the principle of DOMINANCE and the principle that one should maximize EXPECTED UTILITY.

Maxwell, James —*see* SCIENTISTS.

McTaggart, John (McTaggart Ellis) (1866-1925) English METAPHYSICIAN, known for his IDEALIST views and his denial of the reality of time.

mean ARISTOTLE thought that a general principle of the good was that it was a mean (i.e., a half-way average between extremes). Courage, for example, is a good thing, half-way between rash foolhardiness and cowardliness. Sometimes called the 'golden mean'. Students sometimes automatically argue for a compromise between opposing positions, thinking that the mean position is always the best; but this doesn't always make for good philosophy.

meaningful / meaningless *See* VERIFICATION THEORY OF MEANING.

mechanistic Having to do with the sorts of causes and effects we suppose operate in merely physical processes. A mechanistic explanation would avoid talk of aims, desires, purposes, and FUNCTIONS.

medieval philosophy The dividing lines between AN-CIENT, medieval, and MODERN PHILOSOPHY are rough, but it's often said that medieval philosophy starts with St. AUGUSTINE (about A.D. 400), and ends just before DES-CARTES (about A.D. 1600). Some of the best-known medieval philosophers are ABELARD, ANSELM, BOETHIUS, DUNS SCOTUS, OCKHAM, and THOMAS AQUINAS. [sometimes spelled 'mediaeval']

Meinong, Alexius (1853-1920) Austrian philosopher; developed BRENTANO's views on the different sorts of "existence" of the objects of thought.

members of a set *See* SET.

mention / use If you heard someone say "The pig is short," you might be unsure whether he meant that a pig is not tall, or that the phrase 'the pig' is a short phrase. If he was saying the first, then he was *using* the term 'the pig'; if the second, then he was *mentioning* it. Had he said "The phrase 'the pig' is short" then it would have been unambiguous that he was mentioning that phrase, not using it. In written English, ambiguity can be eliminated by putting the mentioned part in quotes: 'The pig' is short. A frequent philosophical custom is to put mentioned bits of language into single quotes—that has been done in this dictionary. Double quotes are used for reporting what someone said (and for other uses).

Merleau-Ponty, Maurice (1908-1961) French PHENOMENOLOGIST / EXISTENTIALIST, follower of HUS-SERL. Known for his applications of PHENOMENOLOGI-CAL methods to perception and language.

meta- This prefix often means 'beyond', or 'about', so thinking about meta-x is (sometimes) thinking about the structure or nature of x. Examples of its use are

'METALANGUAGE' and 'metaethics'(*see* NORMATIVE / DESCRIPTIVE); it is used differently, however, in 'METAPHYSICS'.

metaethics *See* NORMATIVE / DESCRIPTIVE.

metalanguage / object language A metalanguage is a language used in talking about another language. In LOGIC, one distinguishes between the object language and the metalanguage. Thus, for example, particular inferences are symbolized in the object language, but general forms of valid inference are symbolized in the metalanguage. [sometimes hyphenated: 'meta-language']

metaphysical behaviourism *See* BEHAVIOURISM.

metaphysics One of the main branches of philosophy, having to do with the ultimate components of reality, the types of things that exist, the nature of CAUSE, change, time, God, FREE WILL, etc. It is said that this word derives from the fact that later editors called one of Aristotle's books *The Metaphysics*, merely because *'meta'* in Greek means 'next' or 'beyond', and the editors placed it after Aristotle's book on "physics" — i.e., nature. In this case the etymology suggested in the definition of *'META-'*, above, does not work: metaphysics is not precisely the study of the structure or of the ultimate components of physics or nature.

metempsychosis *See* REINCARNATION.

method of agreement / disagreement etc. *See* MILL'S METHODS.

method of doubt *See* CARTESIAN DOUBT.

methodological behaviourism *See* BEHAVIOURISM.

methodological solipsism Jerry Fodor's term for what he claims is the method that is (or should be) used by psychologists and philosophers of psychology: one concentrates on what's going on "inside the head" only, ignoring its connection with the outside world. (*See* SOLIPSISM — though this is just an ANALOGY to solipsism, not a form of it.)

micro-reductionism *See* REDUCTIONISM.

middle term / premise *See* MAJOR / MIDDLE / MINOR TERM / PREMISE.

Mill, John Stuart (1806-1873) The most influential English philosopher of his time. Known for his thoroughgoing EMPIRICISM, his work on the principles of scientific enquiry, his development of UTILITARIANISM, and his LIBERAL political views.

Mill's methods Five rules proposed by John Stuart MILL for inductive reasoning. They are: (1) The Method of Agreement: If two (or more) instances of a phenomenon have only one condition in common, that condition is its (or their) cause. (2) The Method of Difference: If an instance of a phenomenon and an instance in which this phenomenon doesn't happen are the same except for one condition of the phenomenon, that condition is the cause of the phenomenon. (3) The Joint Method of Agreement and Difference: Uses both the above methods. (4) The Method of Residues: Subtract from a phenomenon what's known to be the effect of certain conditions, and what's left is the effect of the other conditions. (5) The Method of Concomitant Variation: When two phenomena vary together, either one causes another, or they have a common cause.

mind-body problem What is the relation between mental and physical events? Is one sort of event reducible (*see* REDUCTIONISM) to the other? Or are they distinct? Are mental events merely a sort of bodily event?

minimax *See* MAXIMIN.

minor term / premise *See* MAJOR / MIDDLE / MINOR TERM / PREMISE.

misplaced concreteness —*See* CONCRETE, REIFICATION

modal fallacy A fallacy in modal reasoning (*see* MODAL LOGIC) in which, for example, the premises 'It's necessary that: if p then q' and 'p' are used mistakenly to derive 'It's necessary that q'.

modal logic The study of the features and relations of sentences, involving words such as 'necessary' and 'possible' 'ought', 'must', 'knows', 'before', etc., and of good reasoning involving these sentences. For the basic types of modal logic, *see* ALETHIC, DEONTIC, EPISTEMIC, TEMPORAL.

model A model, in the sense in which scientists and philosophers use the term, is a tool for studying something, which shares some features, in a simplified way, with what is being studied. SYMBOLIC LOGIC, for example, is a model of ordinary language, in that it represents, in a simplified way, the logical connections in language. A scientific theory can explain some natural phenomena by proposing a model for it: a simple and abstract system of LAWS **3** and equations that represent its behaviour.

modern philosophy The borderline between MEDIEVAL PHILOSOPHY and modern philosophy is rough, but it is usually said that DESCARTES was the first modern philosopher (around 1600). The era of modern philosophy can be said to extend through the present, though it's sometimes distinguished from nineteenth- and twentieth-century philosophy.

modes Normally means kinds or manners of things; SPINOZA used this to refer to accidental (*see* ESSENTIAL / ACCIDENTAL) properties or modifications of attributes.

modus ponens (Latin: "method of putting") A rule for correct DEDUCTION of the form: 'If p then q; p; therefore q'. Also called 'affirming the antecedent' (*see* CONDITIONAL).

modus tollens (Latin: "method of taking") A rule for correct DEDUCTION of the form: 'If p then q; it's not the case that q; therefore it's not the case that p'. Also called 'denying the consequent' (*see* CONDITIONAL).

monad A simple, basic, indivisible, impenetrable, self-determining thing. The term is associated most closely with LEIBNIZ, who thought that the universe was to be understood as an infinite number of monads, in perfect harmony.

monism *See* DUALISM / MONISM / PLURALISM.

Montaigne, Michel *See* WRITERS.

Monte Carlo fallacy *See* GAMBLER'S FALLACY.

monotheism / polytheism / pantheism Monotheism is the belief in one (and only one) God. Polytheism is the belief in many gods. Pantheism is the belief that God somehow exists in everything, or that everything is God.

Montesquieu, Baron de *See* WRITERS.

Moore, G(eorge) E(dward) (1873-1958) English (Cambridge) philosopher; led the revolt early in this century against IDEALISM; the father of ANALYTIC PHILOSOPHY; a frequent defender of common sense against abstruse philosophical theory and PARADOX, and for a philosophical method based on clarification and analysis of meanings.

moral argument for God's existence Here is one version of this ARGUMENT:

> There is a real objective difference between right and wrong, but the only way to make sense of this is to think of it as arising from God's will. So the existence of morality shows that God exists.

> Critics of this argument dispute its premise that morality is objective, or its premise that the only sense that can be made of objective morality is to think of it as God's will.

moral dilemma *See* DILEMMA.

moralities, act / agent *See* ACT / AGENT MORALITIES.

morality One's morality is one's tendency to do right or wrong, or one's beliefs about what's right and wrong, good and bad. 'Morality' and 'ethics' (and 'moral' and 'ethical') are usually used as synonyms, though the second, not the first, is generally used as the name of the philosophical study of these matters (*see* NORMATIVE / DESCRIPTIVE). Philosophers usually avoid the tendency in ordinary talk to restrict the word 'ethics' to an official code of acceptable behaviour in some area (as in 'professional ethics').

morality, slave / master *See* SLAVE / MASTER MORALITY.

moral responsibility *See* RESPONSIBILITY.

mover, unmoved *See* UNMOVED MOVER.

Müller-Lyer illusion An optical ILLUSION (named for the German philosopher Franz Müller-Lyer, 1857-1916) in which two lines of equal length appear different in length. A standard illusion useful in the philosophy of perception. Other drawings often used as philosophical examples are the Necker (reversing) cube, which reverses as you stare at it, and the duck-rabbit, which can be seen as a representation of a duck or of a rabbit. WITTGENSTEIN used this in his discussion of "seeing-as.")

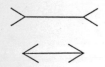

multi-valued logic *See* MANY-VALUED LOGIC.

mutatis mutandis (Latin: roughly, "changes having been made") One says, "This case is, mutatis mutandis, like the other," meaning that the two cases are alike except for certain details—that one can derive one case from the other by making the appropriate substitutions or changes. ['myou-TAH-tis myou-TAN-dis']

mutually exclusive / jointly exhaustive Two mutually exclusive SETS do not overlap each other in membership. For example, each item on the list: 'mammals, birds, fish, reptiles, amphibians' is exclusive of the others, since nothing belongs to more than one of these categories. The list is jointly exhaustive of vertebrates, since every vertebrate is included in these categories. It is mutually exclusive *and* jointly exhaustive because every vertebrate is included in *exactly one* of these categories.

mystical experience argument for God's existence Sometimes the existence and nature of the mystical experiences some people have are thought to provide evidence for God's existence. Thus, mystical experience is the basis of an argument for God's existence. One criticism of this argument is that even though religious experience sometimes provides compelling motivation for belief in God, this sort of convincing is not a matter of ARGUMENT. The relevance of mystical experience was explored at length by JAMES.

mysticism A variety of religious practice that relies on direct experience, supposed to be of God and of supernatural truths. Mystics often advocate exercises or rituals designed to induce the abnormal psychological states in which these experiences occur. They commonly hold that in these experiences we achieve union with God or with the divine ground of all being.

N

Nagel, Ernest (b. 1901) American philosopher, with important work on philosophy of science and LOGIC.

naive realism What's supposed to be the ordinary view about perception: that it reveals external objects to us directly, the way they really are. The implication here usually is that this naive view is overturned by philosophical sophistication (*see*, for instance, the ARGUMENT FROM ILLUSION). Also called common-sense realism. ['naïve' is sometimes spelled with those two dots over the 'i']

natural Be very careful when using this word—it has a variety of meanings. It can mean "pertaining to nature" (in the narrow sense of trees and bugs, or in the wider sense as contrasted with what we create), 'original', 'PRIMITIVE', 'spontaneous', 'undisguised', 'physical', 'INNATE', 'usual', 'accepted', or 'the way things ought to be'.

natural / conventional rights *See* RIGHTS.

natural deduction Natural DEDUCTION is a system for DERIVATION supposed to match relatively closely the ways we actually think.

natural kind We can see the world as divided into all sorts of categories, but many philosophers think that only some of these divisions correspond to the way nature really is divided. The category named by 'things within fifty miles of the Eiffel Tower', for example, is an artificial kind, one invented by us; but sorting out things by difference in mass might be supposed to be a categorization that is in nature — one that is important for CAUSE and effect, and that will figure in real science. Categories like this, that "cut nature at the joints," are called 'natural kinds'. NOMINALISTS think there are no natural kinds — all kinds are artificial — though they agree that some sorts of categorizations will be more important in science than others. Scientific REALISTS who believe in natural kinds need to explain what makes a kind one of these. (*See also* UNIVERSALS)

natural languages *See* ARTIFICIAL / NATURAL LAN-GUAGES.

naturalism / nonnaturalism / supernaturalism, ethical *See* ETHICAL NATURALISM / NONNATURALISM / SUPERNATURALISM.

natural law There are several philosophically relevant senses of this phrase. Its ambiguity is due partly to the variety of meanings of 'LAW'. A natural law can be: **1.** A law of nature — i.e., a formulation of a regularity found in the natural world, the sort of thing science discovers. **2.** A principle of proper human action or conduct, taken to be God-given, or to be a consequence of "human nature" — our structure or function. In this sense, there are "natural law" theories in ethics and in political philosophy. THOMAS AQUINAS is perhaps the philosopher most closely associated with these. **3.** The name of a theory of societal law that holds that the validity of the laws of a legal system depends on their coherence with God-given or otherwise objective morality; it says, in other words, that social law depends on natural law in sense 2, just above.

naturalism, ethical *See* ETHICAL NATURALISM / SUPER-
NATURALISM / NONNATURALISM.

naturalistic fallacy The supposed mistake in reasoning
that springs from the ASSUMPTION **2** that ethical words
can be defined in terms of natural ones, ethical nonnaturalists such as MOORE claim to detect this fallacy in
the thought of ethical naturalists. *See* ETHICAL
NATURALISM / SUPERNATURALISM / NONNATURALISM,
OPEN QUESTION ARGUMENT.

natural philosophy *See* SCIENCE.

natural selection *See* EVOLUTION.

nature, state of *See* STATE OF NATURE.

necessary / contingent truth The word 'necessary' has
a special use in philosophy, different from its ordinary
sense. We say things like 'It's necessary that I go to the
bathroom', but in philosophy a necessary truth is a statement that is true and could not possibly be false; a contingent truth could be false (but isn't, just as a matter of
fact). Such statements as '7 + 5 = 12' and 'All bachelors
are unmarried' and 'Every event has a cause' are often
thought to be necessary; 'Pigs don't fly', 'More than a
million grains of sand exist', and 'The Earth is bigger
than Mars' are contingent truths. (Similarly, there are
necessary and contingent falsehoods.) Many
philosophers think that the necessity or contingency of
some fact is a METAPHYSICAL matter – is a matter of the
way the external world is – but some philosophers think
that this difference is merely a matter of the way we think
or talk about the world – that a truth taken to be necessary is merely a CONCEPTUAL or LOGICAL or ANALYTIC
TRUTH (*see also* LOGICISM). 'Contingent' is sometimes
also used to contrast with 'LOGICALLY TRUE / FALSE'. A

necessary truth is also called a 'necessity', and a contingent truth a 'contingency'.

necessary / sufficient condition X is a sufficient condition for Y when: if X is true, then Y must also be true. This is the same as saying: X can't be without Y. For example, the fact that something is a pig is sufficient for that thing to be an animal. X is a necessary condition for Y when: if Y is true, then X must also be true. In other words, Y can't be without X. Thus the fact that something is a pig is not necessary for that thing to be an animal, for something can be an animal but not a pig. But the fact that something is an animal is necessary for something to be a pig. X is necessary and sufficient for Y when both are true: if X is true, Y is true, and if Y is true, X is true. In other words, you can't have one without the other. Thus, the complex condition that something is flammable, heated above a certain temperature, and in the presence of oxygen is (roughly—perhaps you can think of exceptions) necessary and sufficient for the thing to catch on fire. Saying that X is sufficient for Y is the same thing as saying the conditional statement 'If X then Y', and saying that X is necessary for Y is the same as saying 'If Y then X' (*see* CONDITIONAL).

Necker cube *See* MÜLLER-LYER ILLUSION.

negation The negation of a sentence is obtained by putting 'It's not the case that' in front of it (or by removing that phrase). Negation is often symbolized by the tilde ($\sim$). (*see* SYMBOLS OF SENTENTIAL LOGIC).

neo- This prefix means 'new' or 'a later version of'. It is often put in front of the name of some philosophical movement to signify a later movement based on the earlier one, but including significant changes, for example, 'neo-PLATONISM', 'neo-KANTIAN'.

Newcomb's paradox Suppose you are faced with the following choice. Box A contains either a cheque for $1 million or nothing (you don't know which). Box B contains a check for $1 thousand. You can take the contents of box A alone, or the contents of both boxes. A very smart computer has been fed information about you; if it predicted you'll take both, it has already put nothing in box A, but if it predicted you'll take only A, it has already put $1 million in there. The computer has almost always been right in predicting other people in the past. What should you do? The paradox arises from two equally convincing contrary strategies: (1) What's in box A won't change depending on your choice. If you take just A, you'll get whatever's in there; if you take both, you'll get that plus the thousand in B. Take both boxes. (This is the DOMINANT strategy.) (2) The computer has almost certainly predicted you correctly, so if you pick both boxes, it probably has put nothing in there, and you'll get only $1 thousand. If you pick only A, again the computer predicted this, so you'll probably get $1 million. Pick only A. (This strategy calculates expected UTILITY.) Is (1) or (2) the better strategy? Debate about this puzzle has led to interesting considerations in decision theory and other areas.

Newton, Isaac *See* SCIENTISTS.

Niebuhr, Reinhold (1892-1971) American Protestant theologian and social critic.

Nietzsche, Friedrich (Wilhelm) (1844-1900) German philosopher famous for his attacks on Christianity, LIBERALISM, DEMOCRACY, and SOCIALISM as "SLAVE

MORALITY," and for his advocacy of a morality appropriate to a superior individual, the "SUPERMAN," who is above the common herd and embodies the "WILL TO POWER" — to self-assertion and self-mastery. Hitler loved Nietzsche's aggressive, shocking, and iconoclastic writings, though it is often argued that Nietzsche's association with German FASCISM and militarism is unjustified. ['NEE-chuh', though often carelessly pronounced 'NEE-chee']

nihilism The name of various sorts of negative belief: that nothing can be known, or that nothing generally accepted in science, religion, or ethics is correct, or that the current social order is worthless, or that nothing in our lives has any value. ['NY-' or 'NEE-' + 'al-izm' or 'hill-izm']

nirvana The state of enlightenment thought by Buddhists to occur when the self is extinguished.

nomic Means 'having to do with LAW 3'. A nomic regularity is distinguished from a mere (accidental) regularity or coincidence, in that the first represents a law of nature. One way this difference is explained is by saying that a nomic regularity supports COUNTERFACTUALS: it's not only the case that all A's are B's, but it's also the case that if something were an A, it would be a B. [synonym: 'nomological']

nominalism *See* UNIVERSALS.

nomological *See* NOMIC.

nomos *See* PHYSIS / NOMOS.

nonbeing *See* NOTHING.

noncognitivism *See* COGNITIVISM / NONCOGNITIVISM.

nonnaturalism *See* ETHICAL NATURALISM / NON-NATURALISM / SUPERNATURALISM.

nonreflexive *See* REFLEXIVE / IRREFLEXIVE / NON-REFLEXIVE.

nonsense *See* MEANINGFUL / MEANINGLESS.

non sequitur (Latin: "it does not follow") An ARGUMENT in which the conclusion is not supported by the premises, or a statement that is supposed to follow logically from some others but does not. ['non SEK-wuh-ter']

nonsymmetric *See* SYMMETRIC / ASYMMETRIC / NON-SYMMETRIC.

nontransitive *See* TRANSITIVE / INTRANSITIVE / NON-TRANSITIVE.

norm Standard for morally correct action.

normative / descriptive A statement is descriptive when it says what the facts are, by contrast, it is normative when it says what ought to be done, or what is right or wrong. (The clarity of this distinction is attacked, however, by philosophers who claim that what ought to be done, and what is right or wrong, count as facts.) Philosophers distinguish between normative ethics, descriptive ethics, and metaethics. The first is supposed to tell us what's right and wrong, good and bad; the second, what this or that person or group believes is right, etc., and the third, what sort of meaning ethical statements have, and what sort of JUSTIFICATION they might have.

notation, Polish *See* POLISH NOTATION.

nothing Non-existence, non-being. Sometimes philosophers wondered whether there could be perfectly empty space, a "void", some argued that the universe must be a "plenum" — filled at every point with something or other. It's less easy to make sense of the worry others had about whether 'nothing' names a thing. Some puzzlement has been occasioned by HEIDEGGER's famous statement, *"Das Nichts nichtet"* — "The nothing noths." EXISTENTIALISTS distinguish "nothingness" from mere emptiness: the former is a perceived lack of being — a gap that we might find where we need or expect or would think of something.

noumena *See* PHENOMENA / NOUMENA.

nous A Greek term that refers to the rational part of the mind or to a principle of rational ordering, especially as thought to be a causal or explanatory factor in the way things are. ['noose']

null set *See* SET.

numbers, law of large *See* LAW OF LARGE NUMBERS.

numerical identity *See* IDENTITY.

O

objectivism 1. The opposite of RELATIVISM. **2.** The opposite of SUBJECTIVISM. **3.** The position of Ayn Rand, the contemporary American novelist known for her LIBERTARIAN and individualistic political and ethical views.

object language *See* METALANGUAGE / OBJECT LANGUAGE.

obligation Generally, something one morally must do, a synonym for 'duty'. What one *must* do is perhaps not all there is to morality, since some good things are not obligations. It might be thought good, for example, to go out of your way to help a random stranger in a small, unexpected, and unusual way, but it is not obligatory: no one would blame you if you didn't. Actions that are good but not obligatory are called 'supererogatory' — above and beyond the call of duty.

obverse *See* CONVERSE / OBVERSE.

occasionalism Occasionalists hold that matter is inert, so the force needed to move things does not come from within them, but from God, who is constantly intervening in the world to bring about change. Occasionalists about mind and body deny that the two interact: they are arranged by God on each occasion to move in parallel. Occasionalism is associated with MALEBRANCHE. *See also*: PARALLELISM, PRE-ESTABLISHED HARMONY.

Ockham (or Occam), William of (1285?-?1349) English theologian, known for his nominalism (*see* UNIVERSALS) and for OCKHAM'S RAZOR. His work was largely in LOGIC and theory of meaning.

Ockham's razor (or Occam's) A general principle of EXPLANATION that says that, everything else being equal, the correct or preferable explanation is the one that is simpler — i.e., that needs fewer basic principles or fewer explanatory entities. Named for William of OCKHAM.

omissions and acts *See* ACTS / OMISSIONS.

omnibenevolent Totally, perfectly good and desiring the good. Often thought to be a characteristic of God.

omnipotent All-powerful, able to do anything. Often thought to be a characteristic of God, though some philosophers wonder whether this notion makes sense: could God make a contradiction true, or change the past, or manufacture a stone too heavy for Him to lift?

omnipresent Everywhere at once, or influential in everything. Pantheists (*see* MONOTHEISM / POLYTHEISM / PANTHEISM) sometimes believe that God is omnipresent.

omniscient All-knowing. Often thought to be a characteristic of God. To be omniscient is to know everything not only past and present, but also future. ['om-NISH-ent']

ontological Means 'having to do with existence' (*See* ONTOLOGY).

ontological argument for God's existence A variety of arguments that rely on the CONCEPT of God to prove

His existence. In the best-known version it is supposed that part of the concept of God is that He is perfect: since something would not be perfect if it did not exist, it follows that God exists. A famous version of the ontological argument is due to ANSELM.

ontological parsimony The characteristic a THEORY has when it relies on a comparatively small number of basic kinds of things, or a minimum of THEORETICAL ENTITIES. Often thought to be a valuable characteristic for a theory to have, and sometimes thought to provide rational grounds for choice between competing, otherwise equally good, theories. *See also* OCKHAM'S RAZOR.

ontological relativism A relativistic (*see* RELATIVISM / ABSOLUTISM) position about ONTOLOGY. Ontological relativists hold that there is no external fact about what sorts of basic things exist: we decide how we are going to categorize things, and what sorts of things we will count as basic, depending on context and what way of thinking suits us.

ontology The philosophical study of EXISTENCE or being. Typical questions are: What basic sorts of things exist? What are the basic things out of which others are composed? How are things related to each other? The ontology of a THEORY is the list of the sorts of things whose existence is PRESUPPOSED by that theory.

opaque / transparent A transparent CONTEXT is that part of a sentence surrounding a TERM **2** (a noun or noun phrase), which is such that any other term referring to the same thing may be replaced in it SALVA VERITATE, i.e., without changing the truth or falsity of the sentence. For example, consider the true sentence

Terry kicked Fran's cat.

Now, we may replace the term 'Fran's cat' with any other term referring to the same thing, and the sentence will still be true. For example, Fran's cat is named Tabitha, so

Terry kicked Tabitha

must also be true. The context 'Terry kicked ' is transparent. Compare, however, a context inside quotation marks, for example, this sentence is true:

Terry said, "To hell with Tabitha!"

But this is false:

Terry said, "To hell with Fran's cat!"

Quotational contexts are opaque, that is, terms cannot always be replaced without changing the truth or falsity of the original sentence. It is often thought that belief contexts are opaque: thus, if Terry doesn't know that Fran's cat is also Bob's cat, then

Terry believes Fran's cat is here

might be true, while

Terry believes Bob's cat is here

is false.

open question argument An argument against ethical naturalism (*see* ETHICAL NATURALISM / SUPER-NATURALISM / NONNATURALISM) due to G. E. MOORE. Ethical naturalists suppose that an ethical term is synonymous with some natural term, for example, that 'the right action' is synonymous with 'the action that produces the greatest happiness'. But Moore argued against this synonymy (and any synonymy with a natural PREDICATE 1) by claiming that one might be convinced that an action produced the greatest happiness, while still finding that it was an open question (not a question thereby settled) whether that action was the right action.

open sentence *See* SYMBOLS OF QUANTIFIER LOGIC.

operational definition *See* DEFINITION.

operationalism / instrumentalism Operationalism is the view that scientific CONCEPTS are to be defined in terms of experimental procedures, and that the meaning of these terms is given by these procedures. Operationalists argue that any terms not definable in this way should be eliminated from science as meaningless. For example, to be an operationalist about the tiny particles physics talks about is to think that there's nothing we mean by saying they exist except that certain kinds of visible effects exist under certain experimental conditions, and that certain results will be obtained when certain measurement procedures are carried out. Instrumentalism shares with operationalism the view that one should understand what scientific theory says in terms of experimental procedures and predictions. The difference is that operationalists are REALISTS about the objects scientific theory talks about: they say that electrons, for example, really exist, and statements about them are (sometimes) true. Instrumentalists, by contrast, are anti-realists. They say that the THEORETICAL ENTITIES in science don't really exist, and that theoretical statements don't really have TRUTH-VALUE; such statements are actually only instruments, recipes, tools, or calculating devices to relate observations to predictions. 'Instrumentalism' is also the name of the view associated with PRAGMATISM, especially with John DEWEY, that emphasizes the way our thinking arises through practical experience and represents a way of coping with our environment.

O proposition *See* A / E / I / O PROPOSITIONS.

optimism *See* PESSIMISM / OPTIMISM.

ordinary language philosophy A branch of twentieth-century philosophy (most closely associated with WITTGENSTEIN and J. L. AUSTIN) that held that philosophical problems arose because of confusions about, or complexities in, ordinary language, and might be solved (or dissolved) by attention to the ways the language was used. Thus, for example, problems about FREE WILL might be solved (or shown to be empty) by close examination of the actual use in English of such words as 'free', 'responsible', and so on.

Ortega y Gasset, José (1883-1955) Spanish essayist and philosopher, associated with EXISTENTIALISM.

orthodox / heterodox An orthodox belief is one that is officially accepted, or conventional, or traditional, a belief that is not orthodox, or is contrary to orthodoxy, is called 'heterodox'.

ostensive definition *See* DEFINITION.

other minds, problem of *See* PROBLEM OF OTHER MINDS.

overdetermination An event is overdetermined when two or more events have happened, each of which is individually a sufficient condition (*see* NECESSARY / SUFFICIENT CONDITION) for it. Thus someone's death is overdetermined when she is given a fatal dose of poison and then shot through the heart. (Compare this with UNDERDETERMINATION.)

overman *See* SUPERMAN.

P

panpsychism The position that everything in the universe, not just people, contains "mind" — an inner psychological nature. A few of the philosophers whose views are at least related to this position are THALES, PLOTINUS, LEIBNIZ, and SCHOPENHAUER.

pantheism *See* MONOTHEISM / POLYTHEISM / PAN-THEISM.

paradigm A completely clear, typical, and indisputable example of a kind of thing. A paradigm case ARGUMENT is an argument that tries to solve SCEPTICAL doubts about the existence of something by pointing at a paradigm of that sort of thing. Often the reasoning here is: if a word or phrase has rules for use, and fully accept-able actual uses, it must refer to something real. ['PAR-uh-dime', where the 'a' sound is as in 'pat', the adjectival form is 'paradigmatic', pronounced 'PAR-uh-dig-MAT-ic']

paradox A clearly false or SELF-CONTRADICTORY con-clusion deduced apparently correctly from apparently true ASSUMPTIONS 1. Philosophers often find principles of wide-ranging importance while trying to discover what has gone wrong in a paradox. KANT's term for 'paradox' is 'antinomy'. You'll find accounts of some well-known paradoxes in the following entries: Achilles and the tortoise paradox, *see* ZENO'S PARADOX; Con-dorcet paradox, —*see* VOTER'S PARADOX **2**; Epimenides' paradox, *see* LIAR'S PARADOX;

GRELLING'S PARADOX; LIAR'S PARADOX; material implication / conditional paradoxes, *see* CONDITIONAL; NEWCOMB'S PARADOX; PRISONER'S DILEMMA; RUSSELL'S PARADOX; sorites paradox, *see* SORITES; SURPRISE QUIZ PARADOX; VOTER'S PARADOX; ZENO'S PARADOX

parallelism Because of the difficulties in INTERACTIONISM some philosophers were led to the belief that mind and body events don't cause each other, but just run along independently, they are coordinated, however, in some possibly inexplicable way, or perhaps God sets them up in advance to run in parallel, like two clocks set in advance to chime the hour simultaneously. Parallelists thus believe in the PRE-ESTABLISHED HARMONY of mind and body. LEIBNIZ was a parallelist. Compare OCCASIONALISM: proponents of this theory might think that God on each occasion produces the two sorts of event.

paralogism *See* FALLACY.

paranormal phenomena A collection of kinds of events and human abilities whose existence is controversial, including:

Extra-sensory perception (e.s.p.): the ability to know facts not perceived by the ordinary senses.

Teleportation (or telekinesis): the ability to move things at a distance by power of the mind alone, without physical contact.

Precognition: knowledge of events in advance, without the usual kind ofphysical scientific evidence.

Clairvoyance: e.s.p or precognition by a sort of internal "seeing things."

The study of these alleged phenomena is called parapsychology or paranormal psychology or psychical research. Sometimes this study also includes investigation of one's previous lives, ghosts, spiritual healing, contact with the dead ('spiritualism'), and the mysterious powers of pyramids and crystals. Most scientists and philosophers think all this is hogwash. A synonym for 'paranormal' is 'psi' ['sigh' or 'psigh', sometimes abbreviated by the Greek letter psi, 'ψ'

Pareto, Vilfredo *See* SCIENTISTS.

Parmenides of Elea (5th century B.C.) PRE-SOCRATIC Greek philosopher. His central doctrine was that reality did not change and was not knowable.

parsimony Means 'economy', in the sense of 'using restricted means', thought to be a virtue in theories. ['PAR-si-mo-nee'] *See* OCKHAM'S RAZOR, ONTOLOGICAL PARSIMONY.

participation 1. *See* PLATONIC FORMS. **2.** In a DEMOCRATIC society, the active involvement by citizens in the processes of government.

particulars *See* INDIVIDUALS.

Pascal's wager An argument for the reasonableness of believing in God, due to the French philosopher and mathematician Blaise Pascal (1623-1662). He argued: If we believe in God, then there is great potential benefit if He exists (eternal salvation) and very small risk if He doesn't (merely wasting a little time, and foregoing some minor pleasures forbidden to believers). But if we don't believe in God, there is great potential risk if He exists (eternal damnation) and very small potential benefit if He doesn't (some small pleasures). So even if there isn't any evidence one way or the other, it's obviously worth it, on practical grounds, to believe. One problem with this argument is that it assumes the questionable view that we can choose to believe something if it would be worthwhile to believe.

passive euthanasia *See* EUTHANASIA, ACTIVE / PASSIVE.

paternalism Paternalistic action provides for what are taken to be people's needs, without giving them responsibility for choosing their own aims or actions. It arises from a sort of benevolence plus lack of trust in people's ability to decide what's to their own benefit or to act for their own real long-range good. Criticisms of paternalism include the argument that the only real grounds for thinking that something is a need for someone is that that person wants it, and will act to get it, so we're not justified in acting for what we take to be his or her benefit. Another argument is that, even when people can't be trusted to see what they need, or to act to get it, FREEDOM 2 and AUTONOMY are of overruling moral importance. This sort of issue arises most importantly in political theory and medical ethics, since governments and physicians often act paternalistically.

pathetic fallacy The mistake of seeing human emotions, intentions, etc., in things that do not have them. ('Pathetic' here doesn't have the colloquial meaning of 'stupid' or 'dreadful' — it's used more strictly, meaning 'having to do with pity'.)

patriarchy Societal and familial institutions are patriarchal when they systematically embody male dominance over women: when they arrange things so that men hold power and women do not. FEMINISTS emphasize the widespread incidence of patriarchal institutions in historical and contemporary families and societies.

patristic philosophy The philosophy—largely theology—associated with early Christian philosophers, especially the Church Fathers.

Peirce, Charles Sanders (Santiago) (1839-1914) American philosopher and LOGICIAN. Very little of his work was published during his life, and he did not hold a regular teaching position, his views were, until recently, unknown except in the version popularized by JAMES. Nowadays, however, he is regarded as the father of PRAGMATISM and a significant contributor to philosophy of science and logic. ['purse']

per accidens See PER SE.

percept See CONCEPT.

perception In its broadest use, this means any sort of mental awareness, but it's more often used to refer to the awareness we get when using the senses.

performative / constative A constative UTTERANCE is the usual kind of statement we make, saying something that is independently true or false. A performative utterance is one that makes what is said true, as when a properly constituted authority says, "I now pronounce you husband and wife". What is said here is true—the speaker does in fact pronounce them husband and wife—because this act is performed by uttering this performative (when the utterer is duly empowered, and under the proper conditions). J. L. AUSTIN discussed performatives while considering problems about meaning.

perlocutionary act / intention *See* ILLOCUTIONARY / PERLOCUTIONARY ACT / INTENTION.

per se (Latin, "in itself") Means 'by itself', 'INTRINSICALLY'. "This is not a valuable house *per se* — it's so expensive merely because of its good location." Sometimes philosophers say that something has a characteristic per se when that characteristic is essential to it, this is contrasted with a characteristic *per accidens* (Latin; "accidentally") (*see* ESSENTIAL / ACCIDENTAL). Beware of the habit of throwing '*per se*' meaninglessly into what you write. ['pur say']

person Philosophers sometimes use this word in such a way that persons do not necessarily coincide with living human organisms. The idea here is that a person is anything that has special RIGHTS (for example, the right to life, or to self-determination) or special dignity or worth. What characteristics must something have to be a person in this sense? Various CRITERIA have been suggested: having a mental SUBSTANCE or CONSCIOUSNESS 3, being self-aware, able to think of one's past or future. If something like this is what's important to being a person, then a human organism devoid of any mental life — for example, in a permanent coma due to brain damage — would no longer be a person, and could be killed or left to die without continuation of life-support (this is impermissible for persons). Some philosophers who are pro-choice on the abortion issue say that fetuses are living humans, but not yet persons. And it has been argued that some persons are not living human organisms: many have thought that the person (soul or mind) could survive bodily death. If God and angels exist, they are persons. Some philosophers think that certain higher animals exhibit characteristics that give them something like the rights and dignity we have —

thus they might also be thought of as persons. *See also* PERSONAL IDENTITY.

personal identity 1. Whatever it is that makes you *you*. Is it your body, your mind, your personality, your memories, or something else? **2.** In an important recent use, this term refers to the problem of (re-)identifying a person—that is, of telling whether this is the same person as that. For example, what makes it the case that some person you saw yesterday is the same person you see today? Is it that he or she has the same continuing body? Or mind? That the later temporal stage (*see* IDENTITY 3) remembers experiences that happened to the earlier?

personalism The view that PERSONS constitute a basic category for ONTOLOGY and EXPLANATION.

persuasive definition *See* DEFINITION.

pessimism / optimism Optimism is a hopeful attitude, or the view that things are fundamentally good, or will improve, or can be fixed; an extreme version of optimism holds that this is the BEST OF ALL POSSIBLE WORLDS. Pessimism is the reverse of any of these views. Some philosophers argue that these optimistic and pessimistic views are not just ways we might happen to FEEL, but that religious or METAPHYSICAL considerations offer rational grounds for or against them. LEIBNIZ was a philosophical optimist, SCHOPENHAUER a pessimist.

petitio principii *See* CIRCULAR REASONING / DEFINITION.

phenomenalism Phenomenalists believe (on the basis, for example, of the ARGUMENT FROM ILLUSION) that all we're ever aware of is appearances or SENSE-DATA, the mental events we have when using our senses. Accepting the EMPIRICIST rule that we're entitled to believe in only what's given by our senses, they deny the existence of external objects independent of perception. Ordinary "objects" like tables and chairs are thus thought to be collections of these appearances—actual and perhaps possible ones. Thus, this is a form of IDEALISM. HUME, MILL, and RUSSELL were phenomenalists.

phenomena / noumena Philosophers sometimes use 'phenomenon' in the ordinary sense, referring merely to something that happens, but often it's used in a more technical way, referring to a way things seem to us—to something as we perceive it. Noumena are, by contrast, the insensible but perhaps rationally ascertainable things as they really are—THINGS-IN-THEMSELVES. (Thus, the adjective 'phenomenal' doesn't have the ordinary sense of 'remarkable'.) This is a distinction that runs through much of philosophy, though the terms are associated with KANT. [singular 'phenomenon', 'noumenon', plural: 'phenomena', 'noumena'; ['NOO-muh-na']

phenomenology 'Phenomenologically' means 'as it basically appears to us'. Phenomenology is a school of philosophy, deriving from the thought of HUSSERL, and continued by MERLEAU-PONTY and SARTRE. Phenomenologists believe that INTUITIONs or direct awarenesses form the basis of truth, and the foundation on which philosophy should proceed: by INTROSPECTION, BRACKETING, and exploration of the "inner," subjective world of experiences: that is, of consciousness without PRESUPPOSITIONS, including that the external world exists.

philia *See* AGAPE / EROS / PHILIA.

philosopher-king This term is associated with PLATO's idea that philosophers alone can have those characteristics needed for the best kind of ruler (for example, real wisdom and knowledge of the good). Don't you think he's right?

Philosopher, the MEDIEVAL PHILOSOPHERS called ARISTOTLE 'the Philosopher' as a term of respect, since they found his thought so important.

philosophes (French: "philosophers") Refers to the eighteenth-century French philosophers (ROUSSEAU, DIDEROT, Voltaire (*see* WRITERS], and others). ['fill-oh-soff']

philosophy Oddly, philosophers have a great deal of difficulty defining this word, partly because they disagree so much about what they should be doing. The word comes from Greek roots, and originally meant 'love of wisdom', but this definition is very unhelpful. Better but still inadequate definitions say that it is the study of first or most general principles, or of the PRESUPPOSITIONS behind ways of thought, or of ultimate reality. The best way to understand what philosophy is is to take a look through this book, or through a general philosophy text, to see what kinds of things are done. Most philosophers agree that ordinary folks' uses of this word don't have much to do with their discipline: for example, in 'a philosophical attitude'—a feeling of acceptance or resignation based on a generalized or detached standpoint—or in 'my philosophy', which usually refers to a cliché about how to live. Good advice for using this word in the company of philosophers: don't confuse philosophy with what might be written on a bumper sticker.

philosophy, analytic *See* ANALYTIC PHILOSOPHY.

philosophy, ancient / medieval / modern *See* AN-CIENT PHILOSOPHY, MEDIEVAL PHILOSOPHY, MODERN PHILOSOPHY

philosophy, continental *See* CONTINENTAL PHILOSOPHY.

philosophy, natural *See* NATURAL PHILOSOPHY.

philosophy, ordinary language *See* ORDINARY LAN-GUAGE PHILOSOPHY.

philosophy, patristic *See* PATRISTIC PHILOSOPHY.

phonetics The study of the sounds of a spoken language.

phronesis / sophia (Greek: "practical wisdom" / "theoretical reason") The first is knowing what to do — the right goals to seek, and how to get them, this is supposed to come from experience in life. The second is thought about the abstract and eternal — supposed by ARISTOTLE to be the highest function of humans, and (of course) what philosophers are best at. ['fro-NEE-sus]

physicalism *See* MATERIALISM.

physis / nomos / technē '*Physis*' is related to the Greek word meaning 'to be' or 'to grow'. It sometimes refers to nature, the way things really are, or to the active principle behind being. It is the root of the word 'physics'. Nomos is, by contrast, convention or law, *techn-ē* is what is created by humans.

Piaget, Jean — See SCIENTISTS.

Planck, Max — See SCIENTISTS.

Plato (428?-?348 B.C.) (original name Aristocles) Ancient
Greek philosopher, student of SOCRATES, possibly the
greatest philosopher of all time. His writings, which
often take the form of dialogues with Socrates as one of
the characters, contain the first substantial statements of
many of the questions and answers in philosophy. It is
difficult to know, however, how much of this is due to
Plato, and how much to Socrates. Plato's best-known
doctrine is the theory of the "forms" or "ideas": these
are the general or perfect versions of characteristics we
ordinarily encounter (*see* PLATONIC FORMS). To understand ordinary experience, Plato argued, we must first
have understanding of these forms, and this must be IN-
NATE, not given by experience. *The Republic* presents his
picture of the ideal state: not democratic, but ruled by
dictators who have knowledge of the form of the good,
and who arrange things in accord with this.

Platonic The adjectival form of 'PLATO'.

Platonic forms For PLATO, things have the characteristics they do because they "participate" in a "form"
or "idea" (in Greek, EIDOS'), something in the realm of
Being (*see* BEING / BECOMING) that is eternal and unchanging, and exists independently of any earthly thing
that "participates" in it (for example, as a particular
beautiful thing "participates" in the form of beauty). *See*
UNIVERSALS, ABSTRACTION.

Platonic love This notion actually derives from Plato's
theories about love (expressed for example, in his *Sym-
posium*) though for Plato it doesn't exactly mean
'without sex'.

Platonism Various sorts of views growing from aspects of
PLATO's thought. Platonists tend to emphasize Plato's

notion of a TRANSCENDENT reality, believing that the visible world is not the real world, and Plato's RATIONALISM — that the important truths about reality and about how we ought to live are TRUTHS OF REASON. PLOTINUS is often thought of as a Platonist, or, more particularly, as a neo-platonist. [sometimes the 'p' is lower-case.)

pleasure-pain calculus *See* FELICIFIC CALCULUS.

Plekhanov, Georgii Valentinovich (1856-1918) Russian MARXIST philosopher and revolutionary. His thought, developed from that of MARX and LENIN, was very influential on Soviet philosophy until the 1950s.

plenum *See* NOTHING.

Plotinus (204?-270) Egyptian-born Roman philosopher, influenced by PLATO, founder of neo-platonism, which emphasized the TRANSCENDENT "One" — the unknowable basis for all existence.

pluralism *See* DUALISM / MONISM / PLURALISM.

Poincaré, Henri — see SCIENTISTS.

Polish notation A non-standard SYMBOLIC LOGIC notation in which, for example, one writes 'Kpq' instead of 'p & q'.

polytheism — see MONOTHEISM / POLYTHEISM / PANTHEISM.

Popper, (Sir) Karl (Raimund) (b. 1902) Austrian-American philosopher of science, famous for his emphasis on falsifiability rather than on VERIFIABILITY in science, and for his defence of LIBERALISM in social theory.

posit A posit is an ASSUMPTION, especially some thing assumed to exist, to posit something is to assume it (*see* THEORETICAL ENTITIES / CONSTRUCTS). Synonym: 'postulation'.

positivism The philosophy associated with Auguste COMTE, which holds that scientific knowledge is the only valid kind of knowledge, and that anything else is idle speculation. Sometimes this term is loosely used to refer to LOGICAL POSITIVISM, which is a twentieth-century outgrowth of more general nineteenth-century positivism. *See also* LEGAL POSITIVISM / REALISM / SCEPTICISM.

possible worlds This world — the collection of all facts — is the actual world. A possible world is a non-actual world, a world in which one or more things are not as they actually are. The notion of a possible word has been used to explain and explore MODAL LOGIC and COUNTERFACTUALS, notably by David LEWIS, who has recently argued that possible worlds are real (REALISM about possible worlds).

post hoc ergo propter hoc *See* FALSE CAUSE.

postulate *See* AXIOM / POSTULATE.

postulation *See* POSIT.

pour soi *See* IN-ITSELF / FOR-ITSELF.

practical reason *See* PURE / PRACTICAL REASON.

pragmaticism *See* PRAGMATISM.

pragmatics *See* SEMANTICS / SYNTAX / PRAGMATICS.

pragmatic theory of truth *See* TRUTH.

pragmatism A school of philosophy associated mainly with American philosophers in the beginning of the twentieth century, especially Charles PEIRCE, William JAMES, and John DEWEY. (Peirce called his version 'pragmaticism'.) Pragmatists emphasized the relevance of the practical application of things, their connections to our lives, our activities and values. They demanded instrumental definitions of philosophically relevant terms, and urged that we judge beliefs on the basis of their benefit to the believer. *See* OPERATIONALISM / INSTRUMENTALISM, also 'pragmatic theory of truth', in TRUTH).

praxis Means 'accepted practice or custom' or 'practical human activity', used by MARX to mean the union of theory and practice.

precognition *See* PARANORMAL PHENOMENA.

predeterminism An ambiguous term, meaning 'DETERMINISM' or 'FATALISM' or 'PREDESTINATION'. Because of this ambiguity, it's probably best avoided.

predestination The position of some religions that some or all aspects of our future — our character, what we will do, and what will happen to us — are determined in advance by God, and thus are not determined by our preferences, decisions, or efforts. A religious form of FATALISM; like fatalism, it must be distinguished from DETERMINISM. Also known as 'preordination'.

predicate / predication 1. 'Predicate' is sometimes used by philosophers to mean what it does in grammar: the part of the sentence that says something about the subject, including verb, objects, and modifiers of these. Thus the predicate is the italicized part of 'The cat *is on the mat*'. 2. In TRADITIONAL LOGIC, the predicate (or, more precisely, the predicate term is the part of certain sentences that follows the COPULA ('is', 'are', 'is not', etc.). So it's the italicized part of 'All pigs are *sloppy eaters*.' **3.** Most often these days philosophers use this term to mean any part of a sentence excluding a noun or noun phrase: thus, these italicized parts are predicates: 'The cat *is on the mat*' and '*The cat is on* the mat'. In this use, a predicate is a broader way of saying something about something, or of delimiting a group of things: 'The cat is on __' delimits a class of things such that the cat is on them. Predicates may be one-place ('unary'), two-place ('binary'), etc. The above are one-place predicates (i.e., they contain one blank to be filled with a term), '__ is on __' is a two-place predicate, '__ owes __ to __' is three-place. Predicates are words that name properties (*see* QUALITY / ATTRIBUTE / PROPERTY), predicates with two places or more name RELATIONS. Predication is saying that a predicate applies to something. In the sentence above, 'x is on the mat' is predicated of the cat, and 'The cat is on x' is predicated of the mat.

predicate logic / calculus *See* QUANTIFIER LOGIC.

pre-established harmony Those like LEIBNIZ who didn't believe in ACTION-AT-A-DISTANCE needed to explain the apparent interaction of separated things, and argued that God had arranged, in advance, their apparent coincidence of behaviour. *See also* OC-CASIONALISM, PARALLELISM.

premise *See* ARGUMENT.

premise, major / minor *See* MAJOR / MIDDLE / MINOR TERM / PREMISE.

preordination *See* PREDESTINATION.

"present king of France" example *See*   DEFINITE DESCRIPTION.

pre-Socratics The ancient Greek philosophers before SOCRATES (sixth and fifth centuries B.C.), whose thought marks the beginning of the Western philosophical tradition. The earliest on record is THALES (c. 580 B.C.), other well-known ones are PYTHAGORAS, HERACLITUS, and PARMENEDES.

presupposition Something assumed beforehand, for example as the basis of an ARGUMENT. The statement 'He has stopped drinking excessively' presupposes that at one time he was drinking excessively. A controversy about DEFINITE DESCRIPTIONS concerns whether they involve presuppositions: Does the statement 'The present king of France is bald' state that there is now a king of France (in which case it would be false) or does it merely presuppose it (in which case it might be thought neither true nor false)? RUSSELL and STRAWSON had a well-known debate about this question (*see also* EXISTENTIAL IMPORT).

prima facie (Latin: "at first appearance") Based on the first impression: what would be true, or seem to be true, in general, or before additional information is added about the particular case. Thus, philosophers speak of 'prima facie duties', those things that by and large people ought to do, but that might not turn out to be real duties in particular cases, given additional considerations. [usually 'PRY-ma FAY-sha' or '-shee']

primary / secondary / tertiary qualities LOCKE (and others) argued that some characteristics we perceive are really in external objects (the primary qualities), whereas others don't exist in the real world, but are just caused as ideas in our minds (the secondary qualities). For example, the dimensions of something are really objective characteristics of it, but its colour is not really out there, we attribute colours to things just because of sensations caused in us by some other real (primary) characteristics. In addition, sometimes tertiary qualities are distinguished. These are characteristics by which something has the power to produce effects in something else, such as a magnet's being able to align iron filings.

prime Philosophers sometimes use a notation to distinguish between an original and an amended version of something by writing a single-quote or apostrophe (') after the name of the second. Read this 'prime'. Thus, if Definition D is amended, one might get Definition D', read 'D prime'. Further amendment might result in D" ('D double-prime'), etc. A similar convention would call the amendment 'D*', read 'D star'.

prime mover That which is uncaused (or CAUSE-OF-IT-SELF), it's the first (or the basic) cause, the entity that existed at the beginning and caused everything else. This is often identified with God. It is debatable whether it's necessary that there be a prime mover (*see* FIRST-CAUSE ARGUMENT).

primitive In ordinary use, this used to refer to behaviour, cultures, or people that are undeveloped or simple, nowadays, it is sometimes thought politically unacceptable and derogatory to call a tribe or culture 'primitive'. Philosophers often use this word (acceptably) to refer to what is simple and basic in the ANALYSIS of something.

principia (Latin: "principles") Often used as the first word of the title of books. Two such books are called *Principia Mathematica*, one by Newton, the other by

RUSSELL and WHITEHEAD. Each is sometimes called 'the *Principia*' for short. Another philosophically important *Principia* is MOORE's *Principia Ethica*. ['prin-KIP-ia']

principle, in *See* IN PRINCIPLE.

principle of ... *See* (in many cases) under what follows 'of', or under 'law of ...'.

principle of charity 1. One of the principles used in "translating" someone else's statements, in the sense of understanding what that person means by what he / she says. This principle says that we should understand the other person's words in a way that maximizes the number of true statements that person is translated as uttering. Note that if you don't use this principle, you might translate someone's utterances any old way, also that this isn't the only principle for translation (if it were we could simply translate everything as 'Snow is white' and it would all be true). DAVIDSON and QUINE discuss this principle. **2.** Logic includes a similar principle of charity: when trying to understand the structure of someone's argument, we should fill in the details in a charitable way—i.e., in a way that would make the argument a good one.

principle of dominance *See* DOMINANCE.

principle of double effect *See* DOUBLE EFFECT.

principle of identity of indiscernibles *See* LAW OF THE IDENTITY OF INDISCERNIBLES.

principle of indeterminacy *See* UNCERTAINTY PRINCIPLE.

principle of induction *See* PROBLEM OF INDUCTION.

principle of sufficient reason In general, this principle says that everything has a complete or full EXPLANATION. LEIBNIZ argued further that, in the last analysis, God's reasons are the reasons for everything.

principle of uniformity of nature *See* PROBLEM OF INDUCTION.

principle of universal causation The principle that every event has a CAUSE. *See also* DETERMINISM.

principle of utility *See* UTILITARIANISM.

prior 1. Earlier than. 2. More fundamental or basic than.

prior probability *See* PROBABILITY.

prisoner's dilemma A situation in which two or more people (or groups) face a decision illustrated by the following story. Suppose you and an accomplice have committed a crime. The police have evidence sufficient only to give each of you a short jail sentence, and they want to get a confession fully implicating both of you. They separate you, and tell you that if your accomplice doesn't confess you'll get one year in jail if you confess, but two years if you don't confess. If your accomplice does confess, then you'll get three years if you confess, and four years if you don't confess (*see* the table in DECISION MATRIX for a summary of the situation). They also say that the same deal is being offered to your accomplice. You reason that whether he confesses or not, you'll get a shorter sentence if you confess (*see* DOMINANCE). He reasons similarly, so he confesses too; thus, both of you get three years. But something has gone wrong: if neither of you confessed, both of you would be better off (two-year sentence). So this is a somewhat paradoxical situation, since RATIONAL SELF-INTEREST on each of your parts has resulted in an outcome worse for each than an alternative. Many philosophers think that prisoner's dilemmas of this sort are an important MODEL for thinking about real-choice problems in political and ethical theory. [Sometimes the apostrophe is placed after the final 's']

privacy 1. The private realm, in political theory, is that area of our lives (if any!) supposed to be immune from public regulation. Does government have any business in our bedrooms? **2.** (EPISTEMIC) privacy is the supposed fact that your own mental states can be known directly only by you.

private language argument Ludwig   WITTGENSTEIN's argument that, if there were PRIVATE events, we would be unable to categorize or talk about them. For it to be possible to name or categorize something, there must exist rules of correct naming and categorization. Without the possibility of public check, there would be no distinction between our feeling that we reported them accurately and our really doing so, so nothing could count as our doing so correctly or incorrectly. Thus, there could be no such thing as a "private language" – a language naming private events. [*See also* BEETLE IN THE BOX].

privileged access The special way that you alone (it is supposed) can find out about your own mental events. Other people need to infer what's in your mind from your external behaviour, but you can discover your mental states directly. *See also* INCORRIGIBILITY, INTRO-SPECTION, PRIVACY.

probability Something is probable when it is neither impossible nor definite, but likely to some degree. Probability is a measure of how probable something is: when this is given a number, it's usually on a scale from 0 (impossible) to 1 (definite). To say that something is probable may be to say that it has a probability of more than .5, thus, because the probability of a fair die coming up six is about .17 (1 / 6), we wouldn't say that it's probable it will come up 6. There has been philosophical controversy about what it really means to say that an event has a certain probability. Some philosophers argue that saying a die has a probability of 1 / 6 of coming up six means that the frequency of sixes in a large number of throws will tend toward 1 / 6 (*see* LAW OF LARGE NUMBERS), this is the frequency theory of probability. But what if a die is only thrown once? A competing theory, the subjectivist theory, holds that it means that one is justified in expecting it to come up six only to the degree 1 / 6, or that this number should measure the strength of this belief. Probability theory distinguishes between conditional and unconditional (also known as a priori or prior) probability. Suppose it rains where you live on average one out of five days, the unconditional probability that it rains (which might be symbolized as 'P(r)') is thus 1 / 5. But suppose that it rains in April one day in two, then the probability that it rains given that it is April—"conditional upon" it's being April—symbolized as 'P(r / a)' or 'P(ra)', is 1 / 2.

problematic *See* APODEICTIC / ASSERTORIC / PROBLEMATIC.

problem of evil A problem for religious believers: God is supposed to be all-powerful (He can do anything He wants), benevolent (He wants whatever is good for us), and all-knowing (He knows everything that goes on). Evil is what is bad for us, so God must eliminate all evil.

But there clearly is evil. So God cannot have all of these features. *See also* THEODICY.

problem of future contingents The problem, first discussed by ARISTOTLE, of whether a statement about a future (metaphysically) CONTINGENT event is now true or false. If it is true (or false) *now* that it will happen, how can that event fail to happen (or happen) in the future? If it can't fail to happen (or if it can't happen) in the future, how can it be contingent?

problem of identity What is it for something at one time to continue to exist at another time (i.e., for it to be IDENTICAL 3 with something at another time)? Some changes in the world mean that one thing ceases to exist, and is replaced by another, but other changes are counted as merely alterations in a continuing thing. On what basis do we make this distinction? *See* PERSONAL IDENTITY, BALL OF WAX EXAMPLE, SUBSTANCE.

problem of induction Everyone believes that the basic regularities we have observed in the past will continue into the future, this principle is called the 'principle of induction' or the 'principle of the uniformity of nature'. It is difficult to see, however, what good grounds we have for believing this—perhaps it's merely an unjustifiable habit of mind, as HUME argued. The problem of justifying this belief is called the 'problem of induction'. (There is also a somewhat different "new problem of induction," due to GOODMAN—see GRUE and PROJECTIBILITY.)

problem of other minds If you suppose that the existence of your own mind, and its contents, can be "perceived" directly only by you (*see* PRIVACY), and thus that you can't directly perceive anyone else's mind or its contents, this raises the problem of what ground (if any) you have for thinking that anyone else has a mind, and is not, for example, just a body with external appearance and behaviour much like yours. Some philosophers (for example, RYLE) think that the absurdity of this problem shows that there's something wrong with the view of the mental that leads to it.

product of sets *See* INTERSECTION / UNION OF SETS.

projectibility We sometimes think that the fact that all A's have been B's so far justifies us in believing that future A's will be B's. Thus, being a B is a projectible property. But we don't count all properties as projectible: being GRUE isn't projectible. Philosophers (most famously, GOODMAN) have discussed the possibility of finding the difference between projectible and unprojectible properties. Goodman called this the "new problem of INDUCTION."

proof *See* ARGUMENT.

proof, indirect *See* INDIRECT PROOF.

proper names Terms that refer to exactly one thing, but not by describing them. 'Mount Everest' is a proper name, but 'the highest mountain' is not (it's a DEFINITE DESCRIPTION).

properties, dispositional *See* DISPOSITION.

properties, emergent *See* EMERGENT PROPERTIES.

properties, essential and accidental *See* ESSENCE / ACCIDENT.

properties, primary / secondary / tertiary *See* PRIMARY / SECONDARY / TERTIARY QUALITIES.

properties, relational and intrinsic *See* RELATIONAL / INTRINSIC PROPERTIES.

property *See* QUALITY / ATTRIBUTE / PROPERTY.

proposition This term has been used in a confusing variety of ways. Sometimes it means merely a sentence or a STATEMENT. Perhaps the most common modern use is the one in which a proposition is what is expressed by a (declarative) sentence: an English sentence and its French translation express the same proposition, and so do 'Seymour is Marvin's father' and 'Marvin's male parent is Seymour'. (A proposition then might be ANALYZED as a SET of POSSIBLE WORLDS.)

propositions, A / E / I / O *See* A / E / I / O PROPOSITIONS.

propositions, atomic *See* ATOMIC PROPOSITIONS.

protocol sentences Those sentences that express (what are supposed to be) the basic facts we learn IMMEDIATELY by sense-experience.

proximate / remote cause Imagine a series of events in which each causes the next. The first event is a remote cause of the last (separated by intervening events in the series of causes), but the next-to-last is a proximate (near) cause. *See also* CAUSAL CHAIN.

Proudhon, Pierre-Joseph (1808-1865) French political theorist, associated with UTOPIAN socialism.

psi *See* PARANORMAL PHENOMENA.

psychical research *See* PARANORMAL PHENOMENA.

psychological behaviourism *See* BEHAVIOURISM.

psychological egoism *See* EGOISM.

psychological hedonism *See* HEDONISM.

psychology, folk *See* FOLK PSYCHOLOGY.

public / private *See* PRIVACY.

punishment It is difficult to define this word. Must punishment be unpleasant? If so, then a judge who sentenced someone to not-unpleasant corrective therapy wouldn't be punishing. Must punishment be given in response to a previous bad act? But this would mean that a jail sentence given to an innocent person, either by mistake or to set an example for future wrongdoers, wouldn't count as punishment. A continuing philosophical problem is the attempt to justify the existence of punishment, either in the cases of legal, state-imposed punishment, or in personal instances, as when a parent punishes a child. For major theories, *see* DETERRENCE and RETRIBUTIVISM.

pure / practical reason Pure reason is often taken to be reason working on its own, as contrasted with practical reason (which connects facts with desires and yields conclusions about what we ought to do). These terms are associated with KANT, though he couldn't have meant exactly this, since he speaks of "pure practical reason." Also contrasted with EMPIRICAL reason (*see* TRUTH OF REASON).

putative Means 'supposed', with the suggestion that what is supposed is debatable or false.

Putnam, Hilary (b. 1926) American philosopher with important contributions to philosophy of LOGIC, mathematics, and mind.

Pyrrhonism Originally the extremely SCEPTICAL doctrines of the Greek philosopher Pyrrho (360?-?270) and his followers, hence, any extreme scepticism. ['PEER-on-ism']

Pythagoras (572?-?510 B.C.) A PRE-SOCRATIC Greek philosopher and mathematician, supposed to be the discoverer of the theorem about the length of the sides of a right triangle, founder of a mystical religious cult that believed that relations between numbers were at the core of reality.

Q.E.D.

Q

Q.E.D. Stands for '*quod erat demonstrandum*' (Latin: "that which was to be demonstrated"). Sometimes written after the conclusion of an ARGUMENT to mark it as the conclusion.

quā (Latin, "as") Means 'considered as a...'. Thus, one might say that Fred is essentially rational *qua* human being.

qualia 1. = characteristics (old-fashioned use). **2.** = SENSE-DATA. **3.** The characteristics of sensations (of sense-data), distinguished from characteristics of things sensed. The painfulness of being stuck with a sharp object isn't in the object – it's a quale of your sensation. If you see a straight stick half-immersed in water, it may look bent, the bentness isn't in the stick – it's a characteristic only of your sense-datum. The straightness of a straight stick correctly perceived is both a characteristic of the stick and a quale. ['Qualia' is plural, its singular is 'quale'; pronounced 'QUAH-lee-a', 'QUAH-lay' or 'QUAH-lee']

qualitative identity *See* IDENTITY.

quality / attribute / property These words are synonyms. A quality is a characteristic of something, anything named by a PREDICATE **3**. Some philosophers argue that a thing cannot be composed entirely of qualities, there must be something else, the thing itself, which these are qualities of, in which these qualities are said to "inhere." *See* SUBSTANCE, BALL OF WAX EXAMPLE.

quality, essential / accidental *See* ESSENCE / ACCIDENT.

quality, primary / secondary / tertiary *See* PRIMARY / SECONDARY / TERTIARY QUALITIES.

quantifier *See* SYMBOLS OF QUANTIFIER LOGIC.

quantifier calculus *See* QUANTIFIER LOGIC.

quantifier logic Quantifier LOGIC is that part of logic which deals with sentences using logical terms such as 'all', 'some', 'no', 'there exists at least one'. Also called 'quantified logic', 'predicate logic', 'predicate calculus', and 'quantifier calculus'. *See also* SYMBOLS OF QUANTIFIER LOGIC.

quantitative / qualitative identity *See* IDENTITY.

quantum logic A LOGIC that attempts to deal with the puzzling sorts of things said in quantum physics. For example, suppose that a particle is 50% likely to be in location A, and 50% likely to be in position B, quantum physicists insist that it's neither true that it is in one location nor true that it's in the other.

question, begging the *See* CIRCULAR REASONING / ARGUMENT.

quiddity In (not terribly) ordinary talk this means 'quibble' or 'trivial subtlety'. In philosophical talk the ESSENCE of a thing is its quiddity.

Quine, Willard Van Orman (b. 1908) Contemporary American philosopher, author of several important works in LOGIC, METAPHYSICS, and philosophy of language.

quotational context *See* OPAQUE / TRANSPARENT.

R

radical translation / interpretation The process of understanding a language initially totally unknown to you. The notion is associated with QUINE, who argued for the INDETERMINACY OF TRANSLATION on the basis of his discussion of radical translation.

Ramsey, Frank (Plumpton) (1903-1930) English (Cambridge) mathematician and philosopher. Influential works in the philosophy of mathematics and of science.

random *See* CHANCE.

ratiocination A fancy term meaning 'reasoning'.

rationale One's reasons for doing something, or the support for some claim.

rational / irrational Mean, loosely, 'reasonable' / 'unreasonable'. These terms can refer to people, to their beliefs and attitudes, and to their methods of getting beliefs and attitudes. It is possible to distinguish between rationality of means and rationality of ends: a means is rational when it gets you the ends you want. It is more difficult to give a suitable test for the rationality of ends.

rationalism A philosophical movement usually contrasted with EMPIRICISM. Rationalists believe that reason alone, unaided by experience, is capable of reliable and substantive knowledge, they also tend to believe in INNATE ideas. The classical MODERN rationalists are DESCARTES, LEIBNIZ, and SPINOZA.

rationality *See* RATIONAL / IRRATIONAL.

rational self-interest Acting from self-INTEREST is seeking one's own aims. Philosophers have sometimes argued that someone motivated to seek his / her own benefit sometimes can achieve this only by fulfilling others' interests too. Thus they argued that RATIONAL self-interest often involves more than narrow selfishness.

Rawls, John (b. 1921) American philosopher, his work *A Theory of Justice* is among the most influential twentieth-century works on ethical and political theory.

realism / antirealism Realism is, in general, the view that some sort of entity has external existence, independent of the mind, anti-realists think that that sort of entity is only a product of our thought, perhaps only as a result of an artificial CONVENTION ('conventionalism'). Realists quarrel with anti-realists in many philosophical areas: for example, in METAPHYSICS, about the reality of UNIVERSALS, in ethics, about the reality of the moral categories. Scientific realists sometimes hold that THEORETICAL ENTITIES are mind-independent, or that LAWS in science reflect external realities (so are not just constructed by us), or that the UNIVERSALS discovered by science are real and mind-independent. You might expect 'legal realism', by analogy, to mean the belief in legal principles that exist independently of any legislation or adjudication, but in fact, it names the reverse position: that law is not fixed by eternal principles or legislation, but is created, considering special cases and social conditions, by continuing decisions of judges and juries (*see* LEGAL POSITIVISM / REALISM / SCEPTICISM).

In philosophical use, 'realism' (except possibly in 'legal realism') does not have its ordinary sense, in which it means 'free from illusion'.

realism, naive *See* NAIVE REALISM.

reasoning by analogy *See* ANALOGY.

reason, pure *See* PURE / PRACTICAL REASON.

reasons / causes You sometimes have reasons for doing something, but is this to be understood causally? That is, does that mean that there is a special sort of cause for your action? One reason to think that reasons are not causes is that talk about reasons often mentions the future, but a cause of x must occur before x does. This is a controversy in ACTION THEORY.

recursive Something (for example, a DEFINITION or a FUNCTION) is recursive when it is to be applied over and over again to its own previous product. For example, one can define 'integer' by saying that 0 is an integer, and if x is an integer, then x + 1 is an integer. Thus, applying the second part of this definition to the first, 1 is an integer, applying the second part to this result, 2 is an integer, and so on.

reductio ad absurdum *See* INDIRECT PROOF.

reductionism To reduce some notion is to define (or ANALYZE) it in terms of others, and thus to eliminate it from the list of basic entities in the field under discussion, and sometimes even to show that the reduced entity does not really exist. Reductionism about some notion is the idea that that notion can be reduced — can be given a "reductive analysis" — and perhaps that it thus can be eliminated. Reductionists in social science, for example, hold that social phenomena can be defined in terms of the sum of individuals' behaviour, so they would claim that any statement about a social phenomenon may be reduced to talk about what individual people do, and social theory may be reduced (at least IN PRINCIPLE, if not in practice) to psychology (*see*, by contrast, HOLISM). Micro-reduction is reduction to talk about small (perhaps invisibly small) entities, as sometimes happens in physics. But reduction can as well go in the other direction: INSTRUMENTALISTS sometimes argue that talk about these tiny invisible items in physics should be reduced to talk about visible large-scale phenomena and measurements.

reductive analysis *See* REDUCTIONISM.

redundancy theory of truth *See* TRUTH.

reference The connection between a noun or noun phrase and something in the world—e.g., between the word 'pig' and any particular pig.

referentially opaque / transparent *See* OPAQUE / TRANSPARENT CONTEXTS.

reflection 1. The process of calm reconsideration, which may lead to a better view of things. **2.** *See* INTROSPECTION [a chiefly British alternative spelling is 'reflexion']

reflexion *See* REFLECTION.

reflexive / irreflexive / nonreflexive A RELATION is reflexive if everything has that relation to itself. For example, 'is the same age as' is reflexive, because everything is the same age as itself. But 'has a different address than' is irreflexive, because nothing has a different address than itself. And 'likes' is nonreflexive, because some things do like themselves, and some things don't.

refutation The demonstration by means of ARGUMENT that some position is mistaken. Philosophy students often misuse this word to refer to any attempt to rebut a position: "The Church refuted Galileo's claim that the earth travelled around the sun by appealing to Scripture." Something is refuted, properly speaking, only when it is successfully shown to be false.

regulative rule *See* CONSTITUTIVE / REGULATIVE RULE.

regress, infinite *See* INFINITE REGRESS.

Reichenbach, Hans (1891-1953) German-born American philosopher of science, with important contributions to philosophy of physics and PROBABILITY theory.

Reid, Thomas (1710-1796) Scottish philosopher. Founder of Scottish "common sense" school in reaction against the SCEPTICISM of British EMPIRICISTS.

reification The mistaken way of thinking about some ABSTRACT notion as if it were a real thing. Thus, it could be argued that although it makes sense to talk about something as being absolutely (i.e., completely) such-and-such, the way some philosophers think of The ABSOLUTE, as if it were a real thing, is merely a reification. ['REE-uh-fih-KAY-shun', synonym: 'hypostatization', pronounced 'hy-POS-tuh-ti-ZAY-shun'] *See also* CONCRETE.

reincarnation The reappearance of the soul or mind or person, following bodily death, in a different body. Also called 'metempsychosis' and 'transmigration'.

reference *See* SENSE / REFERENCE.

relational / intrinsic properties The fact that something is six feet tall is intrinsic: it would (it seems) still have that property no matter what changes there were in the rest of the world. But the fact that something is next to the window, or is Fred's most valued possession, is relational: it depends partly on the way other things are, and changes just in other things could deprive the thing of that property. *See also*: INTRINSIC / INHERENT / IN-STRUMENTAL / EXTRINSIC.

relation of ideas *See* MATTER OF FACT / RELATION OF IDEAS.

relations Connections, comparisons, or associations between two or more things. Thus 'smaller than' names one sort of relation, in this case a two-place ('binary') relation. There are also three-place relations (e.g., the one named by the PREDICATE '_is located between _and_'), four-place, and so on. The items related by a relation are called its 'relata' [plural; singular form is 'relatum']

relativism / absolutism Relativism is the position that there is no one correct view of things. Relativists argue that views vary among individual people and among cultures ('cultural relativism'), and that there is no good way of deciding who is right. This contrasts with absolutism (sometimes called 'objectivism'), the position that there is an objectively right view. The most common relativist views concern morality ('ethical relativism'), but some philosophers have been relativists about a number of other matters, including the nature of reality itself (*see* ONTOLOGICAL RELATIVISM).

religious experience argument for God's existence
See MYSTICAL EXPERIENCE ARGUMENT FOR GOD'S EXISTENCE.

remote cause *See* PROXIMATE / REMOTE CAUSE.

responsibility We are said to be responsible for an action we do when it is "up to us" what we do. Moral responsibility is responsibility for morally relevant (good or bad) actions; we can be praised or blamed only for those actions for which we are morally responsible. Collective responsibility, for example, of the whole German population for the Nazi atrocities, is a philosophically controversial notion.

resurrection Rising again from the grave. Christians think that Christ was resurrected, and that resurrection of the dead will occur at the Last Judgement.

retributivism This is a theory of punishment that contrasts with the DETERRENCE theory. The latter claims that punishments are justified when they have good effects: for example, the prevention of future bad acts by reforming the wrongdoer, or by threatening the wrongdoer or others with similar future treatment. Retributivists claim that such uses of punishment are immoral, and that punishment is justified for wrongdoers merely because wrongdoing demands it—because it's JUSTICE—or a restoration of the moral order—to inflict punishment on wrongdoers. Retributivists also claim that the severity of punishment should fit the severity of the crime, sometimes they go so far as to advocate that the criminal's suffering should equal that caused by the crime ("An eye for an eye, a tooth for a tooth"). Versions of retributivism are advocated by KANT and HEGEL. It is sometimes criticized as merely advocating revenge.

retrocausation "Backward" causation, in which the effect occurs before the cause. The existence of retrocausation is debatable.

retrodiction Means 'prediction backwards' – "prediction" of the past. A historian might retrodict, for example, on the basis of certain historical documents, that a battle took place at a certain location. This retrodiction can be CONFIRMED by present evidence, for example, by artifacts of war dug up at that site.

return, eternal *See* ETERNAL RETURN.

revelation Knowledge revealed to us directly by God, distinguished from what we find out by using our senses, or by reasoning.

rhetoric 1. Persuasive or expressive, showy or elaborate language, or the study of this. Sometimes ("mere") rhetoric is distinguished from genuine ARGUMENT, when it is supposed that the former is not a good means for persuasion. But there are legitimate uses of persuasive language, so the theory of rhetoric is an important area of LOGIC. **2.** A rhetorical question is one that is asked when no answer is expected, or when the answer is obvious. Some students have the bad habit of over-using the rhetorical question in their papers. Papers are supposed to answer questions, not merely ask them.

right *See* GOOD / RIGHT.

rights You are said to have a right to something or some action when it is thought that nobody should be allowed to prevent you from having that thing or from doing that action. Thus, we can speak of a right to property, or to vote, or to life. Having a right to do something doesn't mean you ought to do it, but merely that you're allowed to do it if you want. UTILITARIANS might be able to justify according certain rights, but usually rights-theorists insist that a right is independent of UTILITY: that someone morally can exercise a genuine right even if it is contrary to the general welfare. (For reasons like this, the arch-utilitarian BENTHAM called talk of rights "nonsense upon stilts.") An inalienable right is a right that no person or government should be allowed to take away. Thus, the ordinary right of those with driver's licenses to drive is not inalienable — under some circumstances, we think it's permissible to remove it. A civil right is a right that is (or ought to be) guaranteed and enforced by government. (Nobody thinks that government ought to enforce all our rights, I have the right to whistle in the shower, but I don't want or need government enforcement for this.) CONVENTIONAL rights are rights produced or guaranteed by society (by government or agreement, or just by custom). Natural rights, on the other hand, are rights we are supposed to have just because we are human (perhaps because they are God-given).

rigid / flaccid designator A rigid designator (Saul KRIPKE's term) is a term that refers to the same thing in every other POSSIBLE WORLD in which it exists. Kripke argued that PROPER NAMES are characteristically rigid designators. Thus, to say that Fred might have been bald is to say that there is another possible world in which Fred is bald. DEFINITE DESCRIPTIONS, on the other hand, are usually not rigid designators, so are sometimes called 'flaccid designators' ['FLAK-sid']. In this world, 'the highest mountain' is Everest, but 'the highest mountain' does not refer to the same thing in other possible worlds. Thus, when we say 'Mount Ranier might have been the highest mountain', we don't mean that there's another possible world in which Mount Ranier is Mount Everest (*see* COUNTERFACTUALS).

Romanticism The name of a wide variety of cultural and philosophical movements associated with the period from the late eighteenth through the mid-nineteenth century. Philosophically, this is associated with the distrust of rationality and ANALYSIS, and is thought of as a reaction against earlier ENLIGHTENMENT thought. SCHOPENHAUER is a good example of a Romantic philosopher.

Rousseau, Jean-Jacques (1712-1778) French Enlightenment philosopher, responsible for important works in moral theory and for the view that society corrupts the natural nobility of humans, and derives its legitimacy from a SOCIAL CONTRACT that represents the GENERAL WILL. His views were influential on the French Revolution.

rule / principle Sometimes the distinction is made in philosophy of LAW between a rule and a principle of (civil) law: a rule is strict, without exceptions or borderline cases, but a principle is more VAGUE and may be overridden. It is a principle (not a rule) of certain systems of law, for example, that one can't profit from one's illegal acts; but one is nevertheless allowed to keep the money one has earned while out of jail because of having escaped. Against this distinction, it has been argued that nothing in law should — or even could — be exceptionless, anticipating all possible exceptions.

rule of inference A rule for reasoning from one statement to another, for example, MODUS PONENS.

rule utilitarianism *See* UTILITARIANISM.

Russell, Bertrand (Arthur William) (1872-1970) British philosopher, perhaps the best-known philosopher of the twentieth century. Founder (with WHITEHEAD) of contemporary SYMBOLIC LOGIC; leader (with MOORE) of the twentieth-century revolt against IDEALISM, though some of his views — for example, on our knowledge of externals (*see* PHENOMENALISM) — tended to be less in accord with common sense than Moore's. A controversial public figure because of his pacifism, his criticism of Christianity, and his advocacy of freer sexual morality; because of his views he was fired from teaching positions and jailed.

Russell's paradox Invented by Bertrand RUSSELL. Consider the SET of sets that are not members of themselves. Is this set a member of itself? If it is, it isn't. If it isn't, it is. Consideration of Russell's PARADOX has resulted in some complications in set theory.

Ryle, Gilbert (1900-1976) English (Oxford) philosopher, leading early figure in ANALYTIC and ORDINARY LANGUAGE philosophy. Important works in philosophy of LOGIC and of mind; in *The Concept of Mind* he argued that CARTESIAN DUALISM was based on a CATEGORY MISTAKE.

S

Saint-Simon, Claude-Henri de Rouvroy, Comte de (1760-1825) French social (and SOCIALIST) philosopher.

salva veritate (Latin: "saving the truth") Means 'keeping the truth or falsity (of a sentence) the same'. A TERM may always be replaced in a transparent context salva veritate, but not in an opaque context (see OPAQUE / TRANSPARENT). ['SAL-vuh ver-uh-TAH-tay']

sanction A good or bad result of an action that motivates (or is designed to motivate) us to do it (or not to), sometimes as provided by civil LAW.

Santayana, George (1863-1952) Philosopher and literary writer, born in Spain but grew up and worked in the U.S. His best-known views are that our belief in the material world is actually a form of "animal faith"; he believed that real knowledge involved INTUITION of PLATONIC ESSENCES.

Sartre, Jean-Paul (1905-1980) Widely known French proponent of EXISTENTIALISM; author of important philosophical and literary works that express the view that humans have no fixed ESSENCE, but live in, and constantly attempt to escape from, a terrifying FREEDOM **1**. Though philosophically very different, he and RUSSELL shared some outspoken political views. [the closest English-speakers usually can get to the French pronunciation is 'sahr-truh']

Saussure, Ferdinand De (1857-1913) Swiss linguist and philosopher, known for his work on structural linguistics and his influence on contemporary French STRUCTURALISM.

scepticism The view that knowledge in some area is not possible. Philosophical scepticism doesn't come just from a FEELING or personality quirk: it needs to be supported by ARGUMENT. Someone who holds this view is called a sceptic; the Sceptics were a group of (sceptical!) Greek philosophers, including PYRRHO and his followers. HUME is known as a champion of modern scepticism. Sceptics often don't actually doubt the truth of the belief about which they are sceptical: their central claim is that we don't have JUSTIFICATION 1for that belief, and thus can't be said to know it. [may also be spelled 'skepticism' and 'skeptic'; spellings with 'scep-' are preferred by the British] *See also* DOUBT, LEGAL POSITIVISM / REALISM / SCEPTICISM

Schelling, Friedrich Wilhelm Joseph von (1775-1854) German idealist philosopher.

schema A rule or category that we use to organize, understand, and formulate what we think about. [plural 'schemata']

Schlick, Moritz (1882-1936) German founder of the VIENNA CIRCLE, leading figure in the development of LOGICAL POSITIVISM. Killed by one of his students.

scholasticism Characterizes MEDIEVAL philosophy (done by the scholastics—"schoolmen"—teachers in medieval European universities), especially the ARISTOTELIAN Christian THEOLOGY typical of the time. AUGUSTINE, OCKHAM, DUNS SCOTUS, and THOMAS AQUINAS were scholastics. The adjective 'scholastic' has come to have pejorative overtones, suggesting pedantry, dogmatism, and exaggerated formality. Are the scholastics themselves responsible for this?

Schopenhauer, Arthur (1788-1860) German philosopher, known for his emphasis on "Will" in the world—an irrational and blind force behind all change—and for his advocacy of an attitude of detached PESSIMISTIC resignation.

science Philosophers have often thought and written about matters we would nowadays think are the proper domain only of SCIENTISTS, occasionally with strange results. ARISTOTLE, for example, announced that men have more teeth than women, and that the brain was an organ for cooling the blood. BERKELEY wrote about the medicinal value of tar-water. HEGEL considered PHRENOLOGY at some length, and discussed an *a priori* proof that there were only six planets. What we now distinguish as science used to be a branch of philosophy, called 'natural philosophy'; the divorce of the two began only about three hundred years ago, when scientists and (some) philosophers began to think that special EMPIRICAL methods of observation and experiment were necessary for discovering particular truths about the world. Even after the divorce began, however, genuine scientists (Newton, for example) still called themselves 'natural philosophers'. Philosophical EMPIRICISTS, POSITIVISTS, and LOGICAL POSITIVISTS have stressed the inappropriateness of philosophical tools for discovery of particular scientific facts. But recent philosophers of science have emphasized the *a priori* philosophical PRESUPPOSITIONS of science, and the necessity of philosophy (proper) taking into account the empirical findings of scientists, so perhaps the divorce is not all that complete.

scientific realism *See* REALISM.

scientists Many people known primarily as scientists nevertheless have thought and written importantly about the philosophical PRESUPPOSITIONS or consequences of science, so they deserve mention in here. They include:

Boyle, Robert (1627-1691) English chemist / physicist

Bridgman, Percy Williams (1882-1961) American physicist

Copernicus, Nicolaus (Polish name: Mikolij Kopernik) (1473-1543) Polish astronomer

Darwin, Charles (Robert) (1809-1882) English naturalist

Duhem, Pierre Maurice Marie (1861-1916) French theoretical physicist

Durkheim, Émile (1858-1917) French sociologist

Eddington, Sir Arthur (Stanley) (1882-1944) British astronomer / physicist

Einstein, Albert (1879-1955) German-born American theoretical physicist

Faraday, Michael (1791-1867) British chemist / physicist

Freud, Sigmund (1856-1939) Austrian psychologist

Galileo (Galilei) (1564-1642) Italian astronomer / physicist

Heisenberg, Werner (1901-1976) German physicist

Helmholtz, Baron Hermann Ludwig Ferdinand von (1821-1894) German physician / physicist / mathematician

Huxley, Thomas Henry (1825-1893) British biologist

Jung, Carl Gustav (1875-1961) Swiss psychologist

Kepler, Johannes (1571-1630) German astronomer / physicist / mathematician

Keynes, John Maynard (first Baron Keynes) (1883-1946) British economist

Lamarck, Chevalier de (title of Jean Baptiste Pierre Antoine de Monet) (1744-1829) French naturalist

Laplace, Pierre Simon, Marquis de (1749-1827) French mathematician / astronomer

Leonardo da Vinci (1452-1519) Florentine engineer / artist

Malthus, Thomas Robert (1766-1834) English economist

Maxwell, James Clerk (1831-1879) Scottish physicist

Newton, Sir Isaac (1642-1727) English mathematician / scientist

Pareto, Vilfredo (1848-1923) French-born Italian economist / sociologist

Piaget, Jean (1896-1980) Swiss psychologist

Planck, Max (Karl Ernst Ludwig) (1858-1947) German physicist

Poincaré, Jules Henri (1854-1912) French mathematician / physicist

Skinner, B(urrhus) F(rederic) (1904-1990) American psychologist

Smith, Adam (1723-1790) Scottish political economist

Watson, J(ohn) B(roadhus) (1878-1958) American psychologist

Weber, Max (1864-1920) German sociologist / historian

Scotus *See* DUNS SCOTUS.

Searle, John (b. 1932) Contemporary American philosopher known for his work on philosophy of language.

secondary qualities *See* PRIMARY / SECONDARY / TERTIARY QUALITIES.

self-caused *See* CAUSE-OF-ITSELF.

self-consciousness In ordinary use, a self-conscious person who feels embarrassed or behaves unnaturally, as if under critical observation by others. In philosophical use, this often means the sort of knowledge one has of one's self that one gets by adopting the perspective that others might have of one; or else the sort of self-awareness one gets by INTROSPECTION. The EXISTENTIALISTS thought that this self-awareness made for FREEDOM 1.

self-contradiction A statement is self-contradictory when it asserts and denies the same thing ('It's raining and it's not raining'), or when it's logically false (*see* LOGICAL TRUTH / FALSITY). Sometimes (more loosely, and rather incorrectly) a statement that is ANALYTICALLY false is called a self-contradiction: for example, 'Fred is a married bachelor'.

self-deception The process of convincing yourself (or trying to) of the truth of what you know is false, because you want to believe it. For the EXISTENTIALISTS, BAD FAITH is a typical form of attempted self-deception. A problem: can you really succeed in convincing yourself that something is true while you also really believe it's false?

self-evident Obviously true, so in need of no JUSTIFICATION 1.

self-fulfilling belief A belief that makes itself true, or tends to. For example, the belief that other people think you're strange will often make you act strangely, and will as a result make people think you are strange. On a positive note, the belief that you will do well in an exam will sometimes be self-fulfilling, if as a result of this belief you go into the exam relaxed and confident, and thus do well. The belief that you have a belief is self-fulfilling (having that belief makes it true). Also called 'self-fulfilling prophecy'.

self-interest *See* SELFISHNESS, RATIONAL SELF-INTEREST.

selfishness Someone who is selfish is interested only in his / her own benefit, that is, self-interest (*see* EGOISM). This is nasty when it involves seeking one's own benefit only, and at others' expense; but some philosophers argue that the rational pursuit of one's own benefit would necessitate sometimes looking after others' benefit as well (*see* RATIONAL SELF-INTEREST).

self-reference Something is self-referential when it REFERS to itself. The word 'word' refers to itself (among other things). The sentence 'This sentence is false' is self-referential. A synonym for 'self-referential' is 'homological'; this word contrasts with 'heterological', meaning non-self-referential. Self-reference can lead to logical puzzles and PARADOXES; *see*, for example, LIAR'S PARADOX and GRELLING'S PARADOX.

semantics / syntax / pragmatics These terms name both aspects of language and the study of these aspects. Semantics is that part of language which has to do with meaning and REFERENCE. Syntax has to do with GRAMMAR or LOGICAL FORM. Syntax, then, can tell you whether a sentence is formed correctly (for example, 'Is the on but but' is not formed correctly), but cannot tell you what a correctly formed sentence means. Pragmatics concerns the relations between bits of language and their uses by language-users.

semantic theory of truth *See* TRUTH.

semiotics The general study of symbols in language. For a description of its branches, see SEMANTICS / SYNTAX / PRAGMATICS. ['seh' or 'see' + 'mee' or 'my' + 'ah-ticks']

sensa / sensum *See* SENSE-DATA.

sense-data What is given by the senses: the internal event or picture or representation we get when perceiving external objects—or sometimes, as when we dream or hallucinate, even in their absence. A straight stick half under water looks bent; we then have a bent sense-datum, the same sort of internal picture we would have if we saw a bent stick out of water. EMPIRICISTS have sometimes argued that this shows that all we really directly (IMMEDIATELY) perceive are sense-data, and that we only infer external objects from these (*see* ARGUMENT FROM ILLUSION). The term was invented by MOORE. Note that 'sense-data' is plural: the singular form is 'sense-datum'. Also known as 'sensa' (singular 'sensum'). [*See also* DATA.]

sense qualia = QUALIA 2.

sense / reference *See* DENOTATION / CONNOTATION.

sensibilia Things capable of being perceived. Also called 'sensibles'.

sensibles *See* SENSIBILIA.

sentence, open *See* SYMBOLS OF QUANTIFIER LOGIC.

sentences, protocol *See* PROTOCOL SENTENCES.

sentential logic 'Sentential' is the adjectival form of 'sentence'. Sentential LOGIC (also called 'the sentential CALCULUS', 'the TRUTH-FUNCTIONAL calculus', etc.) is that part of logic which deals with the way sentences are combined to form other sentences. For example, 'Snow is white' and 'Pigs fly' may be combined by logical connectives to form such sentences as 'Snow is white or pigs don't fly' and 'If snow is white then pigs fly and snow isn't white'.

set A collection of things (called its 'members'). Set theory is the abstract study of the way we reason about sets. Sometimes 'class' is used synonymously with 'set', but they can be distinguished in one or the other of these ways: (1) A set is any old collection (for example, there is a two-member set consisting of the Eiffel Tower and your left big toe), whereas a class is a collection of things defined by a common characteristic. (2) Set theorists sometimes say that sets can be members of other sets, but classes cannot. The null set is the set with nothing in it — the empty set. A unit set is a set with exactly one thing in it (e.g., the set of first presidents of the U.S.). (*see also* INTERSECTION / UNION OF SETS).

sexism By analogy with the word 'racism', this is the set of attitudes and practices involving discrimination and oppression on the basis of sex, most often against women. The central concern of FEMINISTS has been to expose and combat these.

Sextus Empiricus (c. 200) The best-known ancient SCEPTIC; his central view was that knowledge is impossible.

ship of Theseus A story used to raise a puzzle about IDENTITY 3: Suppose that Theseus owns a wooden ship, which is renovated while in use by replacing one plank at a time; the removed planks are stored, and when the renovation is complete, the stored planks are used to build a second ship just like the first. Which of the two is the original ship?

simple / complex ideas A COMPLEX idea is one that can be analyzed into simpler ideas. 'Brother', for example, names a complex idea that is "composed" of the ideas of male and sibling; but 'green' perhaps names a simple idea.

simpliciter (Latin: "simply") Without qualification, not just in certain respects. [usually 'sim-PLISS-uh-tur']

skepticism *See* SCEPTICISM.

Skruijü, Kristu (Latin name Cristus Scruius) (4th century) Albanian theologian, known for his anticipation of the HEGELIAN DIALECTIC. ['SKROO-you']

slave / master morality Nietzsche thought that there were two sorts of persons, the "SUPERMAN," who thinks in terms of master morality, and the rest, for whom slave morality is appropriate. Slave morality involves cooperation and self-negation, fear of change and obedience. Master morality more positively reflects the WILL TO POWER.

slippery slope 1. A form of moral reasoning in which it is argued that some act or practice is undesirable not because it's bad in itself, but because its acceptance will or might lead to a series of other acts that differ from each other in small ways, and eventuate in something clearly bad. It might be argued, for example, that a city's allowing street vendors on one corner isn't in itself bad, but this might gradually lead to more and more permissiveness, resulting eventually in the clogging of city sidewalks by all sorts of undesirables. This sort of reasoning is a form of SORITES argument. 2. Sometimes, used more generally, 'slippery slope argument' = 'sorites'.

Smith, Adam *See* SCIENTISTS.

social choice theory Theory that attempts to explain the actual patterns of choices made by and for society as a whole, on the basis of individual's choices, preferences, desires, needs, etc.; or to say how these choices should be made.

social contract A way of justifying the LEGITIMACY of a ruler or government, or the restrictions imposed by government or by moral rules, on the basis of an agreement (whether explicit or tacit) of the people involved. It is supposed that people agree (or would agree) to these restrictions because of the resulting long-range benefits to everyone. This agreement is called a 'social contract'. Of course, few governmental or moral rules are actually created by such agreement, but it is sometimes thought that they are justified when people would have agreed, had they been asked, and had they understood the consequences. Thus, thinking about this (often merely hypothetical) social contract provides not an actual history of the origin of these rules, but rather a JUSTI-

FICATION **1** of their existence and of their binding force. This is the sort of justification of rules given by contractarians, among whom are HOBBES, ROUSSEAU, and RAWLS. *See also*: STATE OF NATURE, VEIL OF IGNORANCE

social Darwinism *See* EVOLUTION.

socialism / communism In general, both socialists and communists advocate that there be a classless society, that there be public ownership of the means of production, and that people work according to their abilities and receive goods according to their needs. Both terms are closely associated with the thought of MARX and with the former Eastern bloc countries, though both systems have existed (in various partial forms) elsewhere and at other times. In some uses, 'communism' (especially with a capital 'C') is a more restricted term, referring only to Marxist-LENINIST societies; communism is thought to be more AUTHORITARIAN than socialism, and to use more extreme and repressive measures (one hears the phrase 'democratic socialism' but not 'democratic communism'). In a popular inaccurate use, 'communism' refers to any radical view regarded as revolutionary or subversive.

Socrates (470?-399 B.C.) Athenian philosopher whose debates were chronicled by PLATO. Extremely influential for his "DIALECTICAL **1**" method of debate in which he led his opponents to analyze their own assumptions and to reveal their inadequacy. He rejected the SCEPTICAL and RELATIVISTIC views of the professional debaters of the day, urging a return to ABSOLUTE ideals. He was condemned to death for impiety and for corrupting youth.

Socratic irony Socrates, as presented in PLATO's dialogues, often spoke humbly about his own understanding, claiming great respect for the wisdom of those with whom he conversed, though clearly this was to a large extent ironic or insincere, often a technique to draw out his hearer's views.

Socratic method SOCRATES' philosophical methods as represented in PLATO's *Dialogues*. He proceeded by asking others continual questions, thereby to get them to reveal and understand their errors. Sometimes his aim was to lead them to their own discovery of more adequate views; sometimes, however, the dialogues end with no solutions at all. [*See also* DIALECTIC 1.].

soft determinism *See* FREE WILL.

solipsism The position that one's own mind is the only thing that exists in the universe. Nobody sane ever believed this, but it is philosophically interesting to try to REFUTE it. Someone who believed solipsism would be called a 'solipsist'. ['SAHL-ip-sism', 'SAHL-ip-sist'] (*See also* METHODOLOGICAL SOLIPSISM)

solipsism, methodological *See* METHODOLOGICAL SOLIPSISM.

solo numero (Latin: "by number alone") Two things differ *solo numero* when they are precisely alike in every detail, but are two distinct things (i.e., are "numerically" — quantitatively — distinct) (*see* IDENTITY 2.) The existence of difference *solo numero* is impossible according to the LAW OF THE IDENTITY OF INDISCERNIBLES.

sorites An ARGUMENT consisting of a chain of smaller arguments. This sort of argument is involved in the sorites PARADOX, an example of which follows:

(1) Someone 3 feet tall is short.

(2) If someone is short, then anyone .0001 feet taller is also short.

(3) Therefore someone 3.0001 feet tall is short.

Applying premise (2) to step (3) yields a further conclusion, to which premise (2) is applied again; application of (2) to succeeding conclusions in this way, over and over, eventually yields the obviously false final conclusion, 'Someone 7 feet tall is short'. What has gone wrong? The obvious step to criticize is premise (2), but if you think this is false, you need to produce some height such that a person of that height is short, but a person .0001 feet taller is not short; and there is, it seems, no such height. It's difficult to figure out what exactly has gone wrong here, and there are interesting consequences for LOGIC of various proposals. The sorites paradox has something to do with the involvement of a VAGUE CONCEPT (of being short, in this case). ['suh-RIGHT-eez']

sophism An ARGUMENT that is subtle and convincing, but mistaken. Sophistry is arguing using sophisms. Named after the Sophists, ancient Greek travelling philosophers who taught for a fee, because they were thought to use such arguments. Protagoras and Thrasymachus are two of the better-known Sophists. ['SAHF-ism']

sound *See* ARGUMENT.

soundness *See* ARGUMENT.

space, absolute *See* ABSOLUTE SPACE AND TIME.

species *See* GENUS / SPECIES.

specism By analogy with the word 'racism' (and later, 'SEXISM'), this term was coined to refer to the way we tend to restrict certain considerations of moral treatment to our own species. Some philosophers—most notably the Australian philosopher Peter Singer (b. 1946)—have argued in favour of according certain RIGHTS to animals, and against certain widespread ways they are currently treated. Some philosophers prefer the term 'speciesism'; a substitute for either ugly word is 'anthropocentrism'—the restriction of consideration to humans. ['SPEESH' or 'SPEES' + '-ism']

spectrum, inverted *See* INVERTED SPECTRUM.

speculative philosophy *See* ANALYTIC PHILOSOPHY.

speech act An act of communication done by means of language. The speech act theory holds that meaning in language can be explained in terms of its potential for use in certain ways: meaning is illocutionary-act potential (*see* ILLOCUTIONARY / PERLOCUTIONARY ACT / INTENTION). AUSTIN was a pioneer in developing speech-act theory.

Spencer, Herbert (1820-1903) English philosopher who emphasized EVOLUTION as the unifying force behind all of nature, and as the principle of unification of all the sciences.

Spinoza, Benedict (or Baruch) (1632-1677) Dutch Jewish philosopher. He argued that nature is a unity, equivalent to a highly abstract and all-pervasive God, and that its facts are necessary, and can be derived by a method of rigorous "proof" (as in geometry). Spinoza, believing that humans were part of nature, was a thoroughgoing DETERMINIST; given this, he concluded that emotions such as regret and anger were mistaken. He argued that love of knowledge was the highest good.

spirit, absolute *See* ABSOLUTE.

St... . *See* under name following.

stage, temporal *See* IDENTITY 3 .

state of nature The historical state humans were in prior to governmental or conventional rules regulating conduct, or the state we would be in without them. HOBBES remarked that life in such a state would be "solitary, poor, nasty, brutish, and short." Considerations of the relative advantages of a state where there were moral and political restrictions have been thought to justify the existence of these restrictions (*see* SOCIAL CONTRACT).

statements, basic *See* BASIC STATEMENTS.

statements, lawlike *See* LAWLIKE STATEMENTS.

statements, protocol *See* PROTOCOL STATEMENTS.

stipulative definition *See* DEFINITION.

stochastic Means 'having to do with PROBABILITY'. A stochastic (as opposed to DETERMINISTIC) law predicts outcomes as only probable. ['stuh-KAS-tik']

stoicism The views of the Stoics, an ancient Greek and Roman school. They held that VIRTUE is the highest good, and stressed control of the passions and indifference to pleasure and pain (thus the ordinary use of 'stoic'). Well-known stoics are ZENO of Citium, EPIC-TETUS, and MARCUS AURELIUS.

straw man Straw man argument or reasoning (or setting up a straw man) is a bad form of reasoning in which one argues against some position by producing and REFUT-ING a false and stupid version of that position: a "scarecrow" that can easily be knocked over.

Strawson, P(eter) F(rederick) (b. 1919) English philosopher, leading practitioner of ANALYTIC PHILOSOPHY, especially in its ORDINARY LANGUAGE version.

strict implication *See* CONDITIONAL.

structuralism Contemporary wide-ranging and con-troversial French philosophical school of thought. Its central idea is that cultural phenomena should be under-stood as manifesting unchanging and universal abstract structures or forms; their meaning can be understood only when these forms are revealed.

structure, deep / surface *See* DEEP / SURFACE STRUC-TURE.

subjective probability *See* PROBABILITY.

subjectivism Any of a variety of views that claim that something is subjective—that is, a feature of our minds only, not of the external "objective" world. (The op-posite of 'objectivism' in one sense of that word.) Ethical subjectivism, for example, holds that our ethical "judg-ments" reflect our own feelings only, not facts about ex-ternals.

subset *See* SET.

subsistent entity *See* INTENTION.

substance The stuff of which things are made, thought sometimes to be unavailable to our senses, but conceptually necessary as that which "underlies" or "supports" characteristics we can sense (*see* QUALITY / ATTRIBUTE / PROPERTY), and as that which is responsible for things existing through time despite changes in characteristics (*see* BALL OF WAX EXAMPLE, in which DESCARTES argued for the existence of substance). DUALISTS believe that there are two substances: physical and mental. Physical substance is also called 'material', 'corporeal', or 'extended' (*see* EXTENSION) substance. It's what physical things are made of—that to which material qualities (size and shape, weight or mass, etc.) apply. Mental (or immaterial or incorporeal) substance is what mental or spiritual things are made of, and to which a different group of qualities apply: thinking of something, desiring something, feeling pain, etc.

substratum Synomymous with 'SUBSTANCE', in the sense in which this is supposed to be necessary as what underlies properties. Also called 'substrate'.

sufficient *See* NECESSARY / SUFFICIENT CONDITION.

sufficient cause A causal condition that is sufficient for its effect (*see* NECESSARY / SUFFICIENT CONDITION). Some causal conditions are not (by themselves) sufficient: striking a match is not a sufficient cause for the match lighting: it also has to be dry, for instance.

sufficient reason *See* PRINCIPLE OF SUFFICIENT REASON.

sum of sets *See* INTERSECTION / UNION OF SETS.

summum bonum Latin: "highest good." The central principle of all that one should strive for.

supererogatory *See* OBLIGATION.

superman Not Lois Lane's boyfriend, but, according to NIETZSCHE, a person who represents the highest type. This sort lives a self-disciplined, creative, and joyful life, manifests the WILL TO POWER, and deserves to rule over the "common herd." Translates Nietzsche's German term, *"übermensch,"* more literally translated as "over-man". *See also* MASTER / SLAVE MORALITY.

supernaturalism, ethical *See* ETHICAL NATURALISM / SUPERNATURALISM.

supervenience Things of kind A supervene on things of kind B when the presence or absence of things of kind A is completely determined by the presence or absence of things of kind B; there can be no difference of sort A without a difference in sort B (though there may be differences in B without differences in A). For example, it is sometimes thought that ethical properties supervene on physical ones; this means that there can be no ethical difference without a corresponding physical difference in things, so the physical determines the ethical; but the same ethical property can be realized in a variety of physical ways. Supervenience is distinguished from reduction: when to be something of sort A actually is nothing but something of sort B (*see* REDUCTIONISM). Important in philosophy of mind as well: it is sometimes argued that the mental supervenes on the physical but that mental categories are not identical with or reducible to any physical categories. Thus, there is no mental difference without a physical difference, but mental categories are not equivalent to physical ones.

surface grammar / structure *See* DEEP / SURFACE STRUCTURE.

surprise-quiz paradox Suppose your teacher announces that there will be a surprise quiz (i.e., one whose date you can't predict — you'll know when it happens only at the moment it happens) on one of the next five meeting-days of the class. Now, you know it can't be day 5, because if it hasn't happened by the end of day 4, you'd be able to predict then, in advance, that it will happen during day 5, so it wouldn't be a surprise. But it also can't be day 4, because if it hasn't happened by the end of day 3, you already know it won't happen on day 5, so you'd be able to predict it would happen on day 4, so it wouldn't be a surprise. Similarly, you can predict that it won't happen on day 3, or on day 2. So you can predict that it must happen during day 1; but therefore it won't be a surprise! So the PARADOXICAL conclusion is that it's logically impossible that there be a surprise quiz. QUINE and others have considered some complicated matters in MODAL LOGIC that lead to this paradox.

syllogism A DEDUCTIVE CATEGORIAL ARGUMENT that has two premises. For example: No reptiles are sloppy animals; all pigs are sloppy animals; therefore no pigs are reptiles. Categorizing and explaining valid and invalid syllogisms was a primary concern of TRADITIONAL DEDUCTIVE LOGIC (also called 'syllogistic logic').

syllogism, hypothetical *See* HYPOTHETICAL SYLLOGISM.

symbolic logic The main sort of LOGIC studied in the twentieth century, replacing TRADITIONAL LOGIC, and much more powerful and general than what it replaced. It uses symbols (*see* SYMBOLS OF QUANTIFIER LOGIC and SYMBOLS OF SENTENTIAL LOGIC) to represent LOGICAL FORM, and certain of its special areas are closely related to mathematics.

symbols Philosophers often use symbols to abbreviate logical connections (*see* SYMBOLS OF QUANTIFIER LOGIC and SYMBOLS OF SENTENTIAL LOGIC), and letters to stand for terms or sentences. Using letters this way is useful when showing the form of a complicated argument, or as shorthand when you're going to use them several times, but avoid doing this otherwise. If you merely want to say that a man crosses a street, it will impress no one to say, "A man M crosses a street S."

symbols of quantifier logic Predicates (or predicate-letters) stand for properties (*see* QUALITY / ATTRIBUTE / PROPERTY): for example, suppose 'B' stands for the property of being bald. Constants stand for particular INDIVIDUALS. If 'f' stands for Fred, 'Bf' stands for the sentence, 'Fred is bald'. Variables stand for any individual thing. They are said to be 'bound' by quantifiers. The two quantifiers are the universal quantifier ('all') and the existential quantifier ('some', i.e., 'at least one'), sometimes symbolized by '$\forall$' and '$\exists$', respectively. Thus in '$(\forall x)(Bx)$', 'x' is a variable bound by the universal quantifier, and the sentence means 'Everything is bald'. '$(\exists x)(Bx)$' means 'Something is bald'. An alternative way to symbolize that universal sentence is '$(x)(Bx)$'. '(Bx)' all by itself is not a meaningful sentence – it's called an 'open' sentence, because it lacks a quantifier, so the variable is unbound (also called 'free'). The equals sign ($=$) symbolizes identity: '$a = b$' means 'a is identical with b'. The iota-operator 'ι' (sometimes upside-down) symbolizes the DEFINITE DESCRIPTION, so '$(\iota x)(Bx) = f$' means 'The one and only thing that is bald is Fred'. '$(\exists! x)$' (sometimes read 'E shriek x') means 'There exists exactly one thing'; so '(∃!x)(Bx)' is the false statement that there exists exactly one bald thing.

symbols of sentential logic The symbols used to stand for logical TRUTH FUNCTIONAL connections between sentences in SENTENTIAL LOGIC. The sentences themselves are usually abbreviated by capital letters. The connectives are:

The ampersand (&) and the dot (.), both commonly used to stand for 'and'. 'P & Q' (alternatively, 'P . Q') is the conjunction of the two conjuncts P and Q, and means 'P and Q'.

The horseshoe (⊃) and the arrow (→), both commonly used for if...then'. 'P ⊃ Q' is a material CONDITIONAL whose antecedent is 'P' and consequent is 'Q'; it means 'if P then Q'.

The wedge or vee (∨) stands for the inclusive 'or'. 'P ∨ Q' is a DISJUNCTION whose disjuncts are P and Q, and means 'P or Q'.

The tilde or curl (~) stands for 'not' or 'is not the case that'. ~P is a negation, and means 'it is not the case that P'. Other negation symbols are '−' and '‑'.

The triple-bar (≡) or the double-arrow (↔) stand for 'if and only if'. 'P ≡ Q' is called a biconditional (*see* EQUIVALENCE), and means 'P if and only if Q'.

The assertion-sign or single-bar turnstile (⊤) was introduced by FREGE as the sign of a sentence that was being claimed to be true, and was not merely being mentioned (*see* MENTION / USE). Often it is used to mean that the sentence that follows can be DERIVED from the sentences preceding it; or, if no sentences precede it, that it is a THEOREM.

The double-bar turnstile (⊨) means that the sentence that follows is IMPLIED by the sentences that precede it. Thus {P, Q} ⊨ R means that it is impossible for P and Q to be true and R be false. If no sentences precede the double-bar turnstile, it says that what follows is a LOGICAL TRUTH.

symmetric / asymmetric / nonsymmetric Characteristics of certain RELATIONS. A relation is symmetric if it IMPLIES the relation in reverse order. For example, 'is the same age as' is symmetric, because the statement 'Fred is the same age as Zelda' implies 'Zelda is the same age as Fred'. But 'wants to know' is nonsymmetric, because 'Fred wants to know Zelda' doesn't imply either 'Zelda wants to know Fred' or 'Zelda doesn't want to know Fred'. And 'is taller than' is asymmetric, because 'Zelda is taller than Fred' implies the falsity of 'Fred is taller than Zelda'. Saying that a relation is 'commutative' is the same as saying it's 'symmetric'.

sympathy / empathy Empathy is the power we have to imagine ourselves vividly in someone else's place, and thus to feel or think what that person would. This is sometimes supposed to be the basis for morality. 'Sympathy' can be used as a synonym for 'empathy', though sometimes the former means merely thinking or feeling what someone else does, without the "projection" into the other's position.

synchronic / diachronic 'Synchronic' means 'at the same time'; 'diachronic' means 'at different times'. So we can speak of synchronic IDENTITY — when x (at some time) is y (at that same time). For example, George Bush in 1990 is (synchronically) identical with the President of the United States in 1990. Or we can speak of diachronic identity: when x (at one time) is identical with y (at another). For example, the person you see here and now is (diachronically) identical with the little boy in 1950 in that photograph.

syntax *See* SEMANTICS / SYNTAX / PRAGMATICS.

synthetic *See* ANALYTIC / SYNTHETIC.

synthesis *See* DIALECTIC.

systems, formal *See* FORMAL SYSTEMS.

T

tabula rasa (Latin: "blank slate") The term is associated with LOCKE; he and others opposed to INNATENESS think that at birth our minds have no concepts or beliefs in them — they are "blank slates" that will get things "written" on them only after experience.

Tarski, Alfred (b. 1902) Polish-born American LOGICIAN, best known for his semantic theory of TRUTH.

tautology *See* LOGICAL TRUTH / FALSITY.

techne *See PHYSIS / NOMOS / TECHNE.*

technical term *See* ART.

Teilhard de Chardin, Pierre (1881-1955) French Jesuit paleontologist and philosopher whose thought, a mixture of science and religion, received much popular attention. [roughly, 'tay-ar duh shar-da']

teleological *See* TELEOLOGY.

teleological argument for God's existence Here is a common version of this argument:

> Living things are adapted to their environment — they are built in complex and clever ways to function well in their surroundings. This could not have happened merely by the random and mechanical processes of nature. They must have been constructed this way, with their functions in mind, by a creator much more clever and powerful

than humans; thus they are evidence for God's existence.

The usual reply to this argument is that Darwinian EVOLUTIONARY theory provides a scientific account of how these things arose merely by the mechanical processes of nature, so one need not take the large step of POSITING something unseen and supernatural to account for them.

teleology The study of aims, purposes, or functions. Much of traditional philosophy saw nature, and the universe in general, in teleological ways. Contemporary philosophy tends not to, but is interested in teleological systems (those described in terms of purposes or functions, as, for example, when scientists talk about what the pancreas is for, or about the function of individual organisms in the ecosystem): are they REDUCIBLE to MECHANISTIC systems? How are they to be identified? Teleological ethics sees the aim of actions—good results—as the basic concept, from which the notions of right action and good person can be derived (*see also* CONSEQUENTIALISM).

telepathy *See* PARANORMAL PHENOMENA.

teleportation *See* PARANORMAL PHENOMENA.

temporal Having to do with time. 'Temporal priority' means the characteristic of being earlier in time. 'Temporally proximate' means 'next in time'. Temporal logic is the branch of MODAL LOGIC dealing with sentences involving 'before', 'after', 'never', etc.

temporal stage *See* IDENTITY 3.

term 1. Loosely, any group of words. **2.** More narrowly, a noun or noun phrase.

term of art *See* ART.

term, technical *See* ART.

tertiary qualities *See* PRIMARY / SECONDARY / TERTIARY QUALITIES.

Thales of Miletus (640?-?546 B.C.) The earliest known Greek philosopher, whose view was that all matter was constituted of one element, water.

theism *See* ATHEISM / THEISM / AGNOSTICISM.

theodicy The study whose aim is to reconcile the goodness of God with the apparent existence of evil in His creation. *See* PROBLEM OF EVIL, BEST OF ALL POSSIBLE WORLDS.

theology The study of religion, or of religious truths, especially those having to do with God.

theorem In logic, a theorem is a sentence that can be proven in a logical system by DERIVATION from no premises. In some areas of mathematics, however, something is called a theorem of a system when it can be derived from the AXIOMS of that system.

theorem, Arrow's *See* VOTER'S PARADOX 2.

theorem, De Morgan's *See* DE MORGAN'S LAWS.

theorem, Gödel's *See* GÖDEL.

theoretical entities / constructs Theoretical (or hypothetical) entities (or constructs) are things we do not sense directly, but whose existence is assumed or argued for by a THEORY. Atoms and their components are theoretical entities of modern physics. The word 'constructs' suggests that such things were constructed—thought up—for the purposes of the theory; that is, they aren't real (*see* REALISM).

theory In an ordinary way of speaking, saying that something is "just a theory" is a way of saying that it is just a guess or HYPOTHESIS without proof. Scientists and philosophers use this term differently, however: some theories are extremely well founded. Usually 'theory' refers to a system of interrelated statements designed to explain a variety of phenomena. Sometimes a theory is distinguished from a LAW or set of laws insofar as a theory postulates the existence of THEORETICAL ENTITIES. (The word also has a wide variety of other, more technical, uses.)

theory, axiomatic *See* AXIOM / POSTULATE.

theory of action *See* ACTION THEORY.

theory of games *See* GAME THEORY.

theory of knowledge *See* EPISTEMOLOGY.

Theseus, ship of *See* SHIP OF THESEUS.

thing for-itself *See* IN-ITSELF / FOR-ITSELF.

thing-in-itself Something as it really exists, as opposed to as it is perceived (*see* PHENOMENA / NOUMENA). A term associated with KANT; in German, '*ding an sich*'. For a different use (SARTRE's), *see* IN-ITSELF / FOR-ITSELF.

Thomas Aquinas, St. (1225?-1274) Italian-born SCHOLASTIC theologian, perhaps the greatest of the MEDIEVAL PHILOSOPHERS. Member of the Dominican order, worked in Paris and elsewhere. Most central source for the official doctrines of the Catholic church.

His thought is based on ARISTOTLE, modified to fit Christianity; for him, Aristotle's thought represents philosophical truth, which cannot conflict with the revealed truths of Christianity. Thus, for example, he provided rational proofs of God's existence (*see* his FIVE WAYS), which were adapted from Aristotle. Like Aristotle, he argued that the good life was based on the VIRTUES of reason, but added that these are subordinate to (though not in conflict with) the theological, Christian virtues.

Thomistic Having to do with the philosophy of St. THOMAS AQUINAS. 'Thomism' is the name of the doctrines of Aquinas, or of his followers. ['toe-MIST-ic', 'TOE-mism']

tilde The symbol ' ~ ', used for the negation; it means 'not' or 'it's not the case that'. *See* SYMBOLS OF SENTENTIAL LOGIC.

Tillich, Paul (Johannes) (1886-1965) German-born American theologian and educator; his religious thought, influenced strongly by EXISTENTIALISM, has in turn been greatly influential in some contemporary religious circles.

time, absolute *See* ABSOLUTE SPACE AND TIME.

time travel Interesting to philosophers because it seems to involve PARADOXES and impossibilities. Imagine, for example, that you traveled back to the time when your grandfather was a little boy, and killed him then. This would mean you never would have been born; but then who killed your grandfather? Would you be unable to kill your grandfather? Is time travel thus impossible?

token *See* TYPE / TOKEN.

token physicalism *See* TYPE / TOKEN.

Tractatus (Latin: "tract") The first word of the title of several philosophical works. When one speaks of 'the *Tractatus*' nowadays, this usually refers to Ludwig WITTGENSTEIN's *Tractatus Logico-Philosophicus*, a short but hugely influential book on thought and language. ['trak-TAY-tus' or 'trak-TAH-tus']

traditional logic Logic before the twentieth century. Largely concerned with cataloging and describing some of the correct and incorrect forms of reasoning, including the FALLACIES and the SYLLOGISM. Contemporary SYMBOLIC LOGIC has largely replaced it (except in some logic textbooks).

transcendence 1. *See* TRANSCENDENT / IMMANENT.
    2. SARTRE's term for a person's plans and hopes for his / her future.

transcendental The sort of thought that attempts to discover the (perhaps universal and necessary) laws of reason, and to deduce consequences from this about how reality must be understood by any mind. KANT used this sort of reasoning—the "transcendental argument"—to argue in favour of *A PRIORI* METAPHYSICAL truths. (*See also* TRANSCENDENT / IMMANENT).

transcendental ego *See* EMPIRICAL / TRANSCENDENTAL EGO.

transcendent / immanent 'Transcendent' means 'higher than, existing apart from or beyond'. To think of God as transcendent is to think of Him as separate from the ordinary universe, in a different and higher realm. This is contrasted with an immanent God, who exists in His creation. 'Transcendent' truths were for KANT those that are unknowable, not the proper business of philosophy; he contrasted these with 'TRANSCENDENTAL' ones, which he thought his transcendental reasoning could discover.

transitive / intransitive / nontransitive A characteristic of some relations, such that if A has that relation to B and B to C, then it follows that A has that relation to C. For example, 'taller than' names a transitive relation, because if Arnold is taller than Bernie, and Bernie is taller than Clara, it follows that Arnold is taller than Clara. 'Is a friend of' names a nontransitive relation, because it's possible that Arnold is a friend of Bernie, and Bernie is a friend of Clara, but Arnold is not a friend of Clara. 'Is the father of' names an intransitive relation, because if Arnold is the father of Bernie, and Bernie is the father of Clara, then it follows that it's false that Arnold is the father of Clara.

translation, indeterminacy of *See* INDETERMINACY OF TRANSLATION.

translation, radical *See* RADICAL TRANSLATION / INTERPRETATION.

transmigration *See* REINCARNATION.

transparent context *See* OPAQUE / TRANSPARENT CONTEXT.

triple-bar The symbol '≡', meaning 'if and only if'. *See* SYMBOLS OF SENTENTIAL LOGIC.

trivial Something that is obvious or insignificant, so not worth saying. Logicians speak of 'trivial' proofs in this sense. Courses in grammar, RHETORIC, and LOGIC in MEDIEVAL universities were called 'trivia', though the

subject matter was not obvious or insignificant (and
neither did they study obscure facts about sports records
and movie stars); the word here derives from its Latin
use, meaning "place where three roads meet," and contrasts with 'quadrivia', the other four courses in their
liberal arts curriculum (arithmetic, geometry,
astronomy, music).

truth To define this term is to give a THEORY of what it is
that makes a sentence or belief true. Here are some
major theories of truth:

Correspondence theory of truth: Something is
true when it corresponds with the facts. This is a
commonsense view, but some philosophers have
rejected it because they find that the notion of
"correspondence" is completely unclear, or that
we never have any grounds for thinking that a sentence or belief "corresponds" with external
facts—all we have direct contact with is other
beliefs.

Coherence theory of truth: The truth of something
is the fact that it fits into a COHERENT set: the SET
of sentences we take to be true ones is that set
which fits together best.

Pragmatic theory of truth: Something is true when
it is useful to believe (everything considered, and
in the long run). This doesn't mean that anything
you'd like to believe is therefore true: usefulness is
understood in terms of allowing us to make suc-
cessful predictions, and in general to function well
in life.

Redundancy theory of truth: 'It's true that it's
raining' means no more than 'It's raining'. That's
all there is to say about 'true'; truth is not a

mystery. (There are genuine questions, however, about how we find things out.)

Semantic theory of truth: Truth is a property of certain sentences. Which ones, in general? To give an account of what it is, in a particular language, to be true, one should (in theory) give a list of conditions, one for each sentence in that language, which obtain IF AND ONLY IF (*see* BICONDITIONAL) that sentence is true. Thus, part of the list for English (written in English) would contain: 'Snow is white' is true if and only if snow is white.

truth-functionality A truth-function is a FUNCTION whose arguments and values are *True* and *False*. Thus, a sentence constructed out of two sentences connected with 'and' is a truth-function when its truth or falsity depends systematically on the truth or falsity of the component sentences, and on nothing else (it's true whenever both components are true, false otherwise). When a sentence of this sort is a truth-function, 'and' is said to be used truth-functionally. But 'and' sometimes isn't used truth-functionally, as when it's used to mean 'and then'. 'Fred went to the store and Fred lost $5' might be thought false if Fred lost $5 before he went to the store. It's often a mistake to think of uses of 'if... then' constructions in English as being truth-functional (*see* CONDITIONAL for a discussion of this). 'Truth-functional logic' is a synonym for 'SENTENTIAL LOGIC', in which truth-functional connectives are studied.

truth of reason KANT used 'reason' to refer to our intellect in general, not to 'reasoning' in the sense of argumentation or problem-solving in particular. A truth of reason is a truth that can be discovered by the operations of PURE REASON alone, that is, which does not rely on sense-experience. Thus this is synonymous with 'a priori truth'. EMPIRICISTS and RATIONALISTS disagree on the extent to which truths of reason are possible: empiricists usually limit these to CONCEPTUAL TRUTHS, ANALYTIC statements, and LOGICAL TRUTHS; but rationalists characteristically believe that there are more truths of reason.

truth, theory of *See* TRUTH.

truth, vacuous *See* VACUOUS.

truth-table A diagram used in SENTENTIAL LOGIC to display the systematic way the truth or falsity of a TRUTH-FUNCTIONAL sentence depends on the truth or falsity of its component sentences. The following truth-table demonstrates the way the truth or falsity of 'P or not-P'

P	P or not-P
T	T
F	T

depends on the truth or falsity of its component, 'P':

Note, in this case, 'P or not-P' is true whatever is the case; thus it is shown, by this truth-table, to be a LOGICAL TRUTH. Truth-tables can also be used to prove certain other logical claims.

truth-value Truth or falsity. The truth-value of a true sentence is *True*; of a false sentence, *False*.

Türing machine A generalized and simple form of computer thought up by A. M. Türing (English mathematician, 1912-1954). This machine, rarely actually built, reads a tape containing symbols; the symbols cause changes in the machine's internal states, and these changes cause it to erase and print symbols on the tape. It can be proven that this simple machine can do anything any complicated computer can do, so showing how a problem can be solved by a Türing machine proves that it can be computed. Analyzing a sort of behaviour as a complicated series of actions by a Türing machine is giving a calculational explanation of it. Can human behaviour be given a Türing machine analysis?

turnstile *See* SYMBOLS OF SENTENTIAL LOGIC.

twin-earth An imaginary place just like our Earth. This notion has been used by Hilary PUTNAM and others in connection with philosophical problems. If on Earth, John loves Mary, then on Twin-earth, John's look-alike (call him Twin-John) loves Twin-Mary. But this shows that Earth and Twin-earth aren't exactly alike, because John and Twin-John aren't exactly alike: the former loves Mary, but the latter doesn't — he loves Twin-Mary instead. Earth and Twin-earth also differ in indexical (*see* DEMONSTRATIVE / INDEXICAL) facts. Are John and Twin-John psychologically alike? (*see* METHOD-OLOGICAL SOLIPSISM)

type / token Two different things that are both of a certain sort are said to be two tokens of one type. Thus, in the sentence 'The cat is on the mat' there are six word tokens, but only five word types. Token physicalism (*see* MATERIALISM) is the view that each particular mental event is IDENTICAL with (the same thing as) a particular physical event (e.g., a brain event). Type physicalism adds that each kind of mental event is also a kind of physical event. FUNCTIONALISTS tend to be token physicalists but not type physicalists. IDENTITY THEORISTS tend to be type physicalists.

U

Unamuno (y Jugo), Miguel de (1864-1936) Spanish philosopher of life and writer.

unary predicate *See* PREDICATE.

unbound variable *See* SYMBOLS OF QUANTIFIER LOGIC.

uncertainty principle An important principle of modern physics. It says that it is impossible to know both the position and the momentum of a basic atomic particle at once, and is associated with the view that the behaviour of these particles is not causally determined; it may show that DETERMINISM is not true, at least in the realm of the very small. Also called the Heisenberg Uncertainty (or Indeterminacy) Principle, after the man who propounded it, Werner Heisenberg (*see* SCIENTISTS).

unconditional probability *See* PROBABILITY.

underdetermination Something is underdetermined by a set of conditions if these conditions don't determine how (or that) it will exist. Thus, the striking of a match under-determines its lighting (because it's not sufficient — *see* NECESSARY / SUFFICIENT CONDITIONS). Compare OVERDETERMINATION. Language behaviour under-determines a translation manual, since different equally adequate translation manuals can be constructed for that behaviour (*see* INDETERMINACY OF TRANSLA-TION).

unextended *See*: EXTENSION, SUBSTANCE.

uniformity of nature, principal of *See* PRINCIPAL OF UNIFORMITY OF NATURE.

union of sets *See* INTERSECTION / UNION OF SETS.

unintelligibility *See* INTELLIGIBILITY / UNINTELLIGIBILITY.

unit set *See* SET.

universal causation, principle of *See* PRINCIPLE OF UNIVERSAL CAUSATION.

universal quantifier *See* SYMBOLS OF QUANTIFIER LOGIC.

universalizability True of a particular action when it can be universalized—that is, when the rule behind it can consistently or reasonably be conceived of as a universal law (one that could apply to everyone). The test of consistent universalizability is roughly what KANT thought to be the test of ethically right action (*see* CATEGORICAL IMPERATIVE). The test of *practical* universalizability (not Kant's test) is perhaps what we apply when we think morally about some action by evaluating the consequences if everyone were to do that sort of thing.

universals These are "abstract" things—beauty, courage, redness, etc. The problem of universals is, at core, the problem of whether these exist in the external world—whether they are real things, or merely the results of our classification (non-existent if there were no minds). Thus, one may be a REALIST or anti-realist about universals. PLATO's theory of forms (*see* PLATONIC FORMS) is an early and well-known realism about universals; ARISTOTLE and the EMPIRICISTS are associated with anti-realism. Nominalism is a variety of anti-realism that claims that such abstractions are merely the result of the way we talk. *See also* NATURAL KIND.

universe of discourse Sometimes it is convenient while doing LOGIC to restrict the SET of things one is talking about in a series of statements; one then specifies a "universe of discourse" for those statements. Given the restriction of the universe of discourse to cats, the statement 'Everything is fuzzy' means 'All cats are fuzzy'. An unrestricted universe of discourse is the whole universe.

unmoved mover It is inconceivable to some philosophers that every event has a cause, proceeding back infinitely; thus they argue for the existence of a FIRST CAUSE, an unmoved mover – that which started up the whole series of causes that eventuated in what's happening today. This is usually identified with God. ARISTOTLE thought of the unmoved mover as the ultimate purpose of everything, which draws the imperfect to itself. *See also* FIRST CAUSE ARGUMENT.

unsound *See* ARGUMENT.

use *See* MENTION / USE.

utilitarianism Utilitarians think that the moral worth of any action can be measured by the extent to which it provides valued results to the greatest number of people. Utilitarians usually hold that results are valuable when they bring pleasure or happiness. Thus, their general moral principle is the principle of UTILITY, also known as the 'greatest happiness principle': "Act so as to produce the greatest happiness for the greatest number of people." An important distinction is between act and rule utilitarians: the former think that moral thinking evaluates each act, in context, separately; the latter argue that morality is concerned with general rules for action, and that a particular action is right if it is permitted or recommended by a moral code whose acceptance in the agent's society would maximize utility, even if that act in particular does not. The famous classical utilitarians are MILL and BENTHAM.

utility As used by philosophers (and economists), this term doesn't refer merely to usefulness (or to the electricity company). It means the quantity of value or desirability something has. Often it is thought that the utility of something can be given a number, and utilities can be compared or added.

utility calculus *See* FELICIFIC CALCULUS.

utility, principle of *See* UTILITARIANISM.

utopia / dystopia A utopia is a (usually imaginary) ideal society; a dystopia is the reverse, a (usually imaginary) bad society.

V

vacuous Means 'empty'. In LOGIC, the statement 'All A's are B's' is understood to be equivalent to 'For all x, if x is an A then x is a B'. Suppose there aren't any A's at all. Then it's always false that any x is an A: but this makes the CONDITIONAL, 'if x is an A then x is a B' true (unless one, non-standardly, takes the conditional to have EXISTENTIAL IMPORT). It follows, then, that if there aren't any A's, all statements of the form 'All A's are B's' are true. So, for example, because there aren't any unicorns, the statement 'All unicorns are mammals' is true, and so is 'All unicorns are non-mammals.' This strange kind of truth is called vacuous truth.

vagueness In its ordinary usage, a vague statement or term is one not clearly expressed, or imprecise. Vagueness in this sense differs from ambiguity (*see* EQUIVOCATION): an ambiguous statement or term has two or more meanings that may each be perfectly clear: what is unclear is which one is meant. In a more technical logicians' sense, a term is vague whose application involves borderline cases: thus, 'tall' is vague, because there are some people who are clearly tall, some clearly not tall, and some who are in a borderline area, and are not clearly tall or not tall. Consideration about vague terms leads to interesting problems in LOGIC (*see* SORITES).

valid argument *See* ARGUMENT.

validity *See* ARGUMENT.

value, intrinsic / extrinsic / instrumental *See* INTRINSIC / EXTRINSIC / INSTRUMENTAL GOOD.

value of a function *See* FUNCTION.

variable *See* SYMBOLS OF QUANTIFIER LOGIC.

vat, brain in a *See* BRAIN IN A VAT.

vee The symbol 'v ', meaning 'or'. *See* SYMBOLS OF SENTENTIAL LOGIC.

veil of ignorance John RAWLS argued that JUSTICE might be conceived of as (roughly) what everyone would agree to be the rules of society (*see also* SOCIAL CONTRACT). These rules would not necessarily guarantee each person an equal share of everything, and if you knew that you would be relatively disadvantaged under these rules, you wouldn't agree to them. Thus, he argued that the agreement be conceived as happening under a "veil of ignorance": that you not know in advance which place in the society you would hold. Under these conditions you'd want to make sure that the worst-off (who might turn out to be you) wasn't in a really terrible position.

Venn diagram Diagrams used to illustrate the logic of sentences, and to do logical proofs. They use interlocking circles to represent SETS; areas of these circles are shaded to assert emptiness, and x's are inserted to assert the existence of one or more thing. Thus, one diagrams:

'All pigs are slobs'

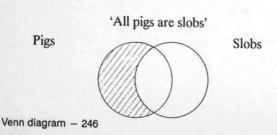

Pigs   Slobs

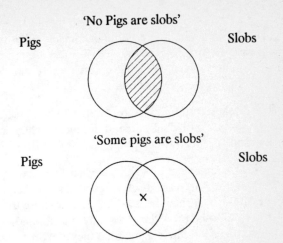

'No Pigs are slobs'

Pigs   Slobs

'Some pigs are slobs'

Pigs   Slobs

One can use three interlocking circles to prove the validity of a SYLLOGISM. Venn diagrams are named after their inventer, John Venn (British logician, 1834-1923); he adapted them from those invented by Leonhard Euler (Swiss logician, 1707-1783; ['oil-er']. Euler diagrams differ chiefly in that Euler thought that 'All' and 'No' statements had EXISTENTIAL IMPORT; so an Euler diagram for 'All pigs are slobs' might look like this:

Pigs   Slobs

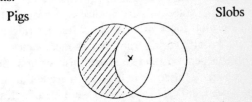

verbal dispute A disagreement that turns out to be merely a matter of words. The dispute about the answer to the old cliché question whether a tree that falls in the forest where nobody hears it makes any sound may be just verbal: the answer depends wholly upon whether you mean by 'sound' an air vibration capable of being heard, or an air vibration actually heard. Verbal disputes aren't real disputes, and are uninteresting unless they reveal significant ambiguities in word use.

veridical Means 'truthful'. Its most frequent use concerns the "truth" or "falsity" of perceptions: an ILLUSION is a false — non-veridical — perception.

verifiability A statement is verifiable when there exist (at least IN PRINCIPLE) procedures that would show that it is true or false. 'In principle' is added here because there do not need to be procedures actually available now or ever, as long as we can imagine what they are. So, for example, the statement 'There is a planet on a star seven million light years from here' is unverifiable given our current (and perhaps future) technology, but because we can imagine what would be evidence for its truth or falsity, it is verifiable, in principle.

verifiability criterion 1. The verifiability CRITERION for meaningfulness was advocated by LOGICAL POSITIVISTS; it said that any statement that was not VERIFIABLE was meaningless. Thus, for example, since it might be thought impossible to find evidence for or against the statement 'God loves us', they would count this statement not as false (or as true), but as meaningless. EMPIRICISTS in general tend to share this position. Some logical positivists used this criterion to argue that statements in METAPHYSICS and ethics were meaningless. **2.** Some logical positivists also thought that verification provided the answer to questions about meaning. The verification theory of meaning says that the meaning of a sentence can be specified by giving its procedures of verification.

verification / falsification *See* CONFIRMATION, DISCON-FIRMATION, VERIFICATION, FALSIFICATION..

vicious circle *See* CIRCULAR REASONING / DEFINITION.

Vico, Giambattista (1668-1744) Italian philosopher mainly known for his views on history, which he saw as a divinely guided development of civilizations along certain regular patterns.

Vienna Circle A group of philosophers who met in Vienna and elsewhere during the 1920s and 30s. It included SCHLICK, CARNAP, and GÖDEL, and was influenced deeply by WITTGENSTEIN. Reacting against the CONTINENTAL ways of thought that surrounded them, these philosophers produced the groundwork of LOGICAL POSITIVISM and were deeply influential on future ANALYTIC PHILOSOPHY, especially in Britain and the U.S., where many members moved during the rise of Hitler.

virtue Moral excellence or uprightness; the state of character of a morally worthwhile person. Philosophers speak of the 'virtues': those character traits that they think make for a good person. Some philosophers think that virtue is the central notion in ethics; this line of thinking derives perhaps from ARISTOTLE. Virtue ethics concentrates on virtues.

vitalism What makes up a living thing? One could argue that living things are just certain sorts of combinations of non-living parts; life is just an EMERGENT PROPERTY in the stronger or weaker sense of 'emergent'. Vitalists, however, argue that living things contain a special (and irreducible—*see* REDUCTIONISM) sort of thing (sometimes called, in French, the '*élan vital*'—"vital impulse" [roughly 'ay-lah vee-tal'] contained by no non-living

void

things, and which drives EVOLUTION. BERGSON is a well-known vitalist.

void *See* NOTHING.

volition The exercise of the will—the power of deciding, desiring, or wanting.

Voltaire *See* WRITERS.

voter's paradox The ambiguous name of two different PARADOXES: **1.** In elections with many voters, the odds are extremely small that your vote will make any difference to who wins, so even if you care very much who wins, there's no point in voting. This is true also of every other potential voter. So it seems to follow that there's no point in anyone's voting. **2.** Suppose there are three people (call them 1, 2, and 3) who disagree about the relative value of three actions (call them A, B, and C):

Person 1 prefers A to B, and B to C.

Person 2 prefers B to C, and C to A.

Person 3 prefers C to A, and A to B.

Suppose they agree to decide on what to do by voting on these actions two at a time. First they vote on A and B: 1 and 3 vote for A. Next they vote on B and C: 1 and 2 vote for B. Last they vote on C and A: 2 and 3 vote for C. Each "pairwise" decision has a majority favourable vote; yet this clearly does not decide matters. This example shows the surprising result that in certain cases even a majority vote of a group does not give a clear answer about what to do. This is also known as the 'Condorcet paradox', named for the Marquis de CONDORCET who wrote about it. It has been generalized by Kenneth Arrow (b. 1921) into the central problem of SOCIAL CHOICE THEORY. Arrow's Theorem shows that there is no rule for social choice that satisfies certain apparently minimal conditions for rationality and DEMOCRACY.

warranted assertibility The characteristic an ASSERTION has when it is JUSTIFIED in the proper way. Statements, for example in science, have warranted assertibility when they are CONFIRMED by the appropriate scientific procedures. It seems that a statement with this characteristic might nevertheless be false, but some philosophers of science think that warranted assertibility is really all that we mean by 'truth' in science; this is a kind of scientific antirealism (*see* REALISM / ANTI-REALISM).

wax example *See* "BALL OF WAX" EXAMPLE.

Weber, Max *See* SCIENTISTS.

wedge The symbol 'V', meaning 'or'. *See* SYMBOLS OF SENTENTIAL LOGIC.

well-formed formula In addition to rules for going from one sentence to another, LOGICS give rules for being a sentence (as opposed to a bit of nonsense). These are called 'formation rules', and a sentence formed in conformity with these rules is called a 'well-formed sentence' or 'well-formed FORMULA'. Expressions not in conformity are sometimes called 'ill-formed'. Thus, by application of the formation rules of a common form of SENTENTIAL LOGIC, we can discover that 'P &' is ill-formed, nonsense, not a sentence (because '&' must connect two sentences). 'Well-formed formula' is sometimes abbreviated 'wff' ['wiff' or 'woof'].

Weltanschauung (German: 'world view') A very general conception of the way things are. ['velt-ahn-show-oong', where 'show' rhymes with 'now']

wff *See* WELL-FORMED FORMULA.

Whitehead, Alfred North (1861-1947) English (Cambridge) philosopher and logician; developed, with Russell, the first modern systematic SYMBOLIC LOGIC; known also for his "process" philosophy, in which change, not substance, is fundamental, and in which purpose is a feature of the external world.

will, free *See* FREE WILL.

will, general *See* GENERAL WILL.

will to believe William JAMES argued that certain beliefs are acceptable despite the lack of good evidence for them, when they are good for us psychologically and help us get on in the world. These are the ones justified by our will to believe them; James even argued that these would therefore be true. *See* 'pragmatic theory of truth' in TRUTH.

will to power The will to power is the disposition to superiority—power over others, but also over one's self. NIETZSCHE's term; he thought that this was the character trait that marked the best sort of person.

Wittgenstein, Ludwig (Josef Johann) (1889-1951) Austrian-born, he did much of his work in England, where his thought was greatly influential on recent philosophical trends, especially on LOGICAL POSITIVISM and ORDINARY LANGUAGE PHILOSOPHY. He engaged many of the technical problems of contemporary philosophy, but is best known for his view of philosophy as therapy, designed to cure puzzles and confusions resulting from misunderstandings of the function of parts of language; thus, he can be seen as the father of

ORDINARY LANGUAGE PHILOSOPHY. ['VIT-gen-stine' or, more correctly, '-shtine']

Wolff, Christian Freiherr von (1679-1754) German EN-LIGHTENMENT philosopher.

writers Some authors known primarily as writers of fiction, drama, essays, etc., deserve mention in here because of the philosophical importance of their thoughts expressed in literary or straightforwardly philosophical writing. They are:

Dante (Alighieri) (original surname Durante) (1265-1321) Italian poet

Dostoyevsky, Fyodor Mihailovich (also spelled in a variety of other ways) (1821-1881) Russian novelist

Emerson, Ralph Waldo (1803-1882) American essayist / poet

Erasmus, Desiderius (original name Geert Geerts) (1466?-1536) Dutch theologian, scholar

Goethe, Johann Wolfgang von (1749-1832) German poet / dramatist

Montaigne, Michel (Eyquem) (1530-1592) French essayist

Montesquieu, Baron (de la Brède et) de (title of Charles de Secondat) (1689-1755) French writer / political theorist

Voltaire (pen name of François Marie Arouet) (1694-1778) French dramatist / poet / historian

Y

yoga The Hindu system for exercise and meditation designed to produce self-control and spiritual enlightenment. A person who practices this is called a *'yogi'*.

Z

Zeno (of Citium) (336?-?264 B.C.) Greek philosopher, an influential STOIC.

Zeno of Elea (5th century B.C.) PRE-SOCRATIC Greek philosopher, student of PARMENIDES, best known for his PARADOXES, which seemed to disprove the existence of motion.

Zeno's paradox Imagine a tortoise in a race with speedster Achilles, with the tortoise starting closer to the goal line. When Achilles has reached the point at which the tortoise started, the tortoise has gone a little further; when Achilles reaches this further point, the tortoise has advanced again; and so on. The ABSURD conclusion is that Achilles will never pass the tortoise. ZENO OF ELEA, who produced this PARADOX, concluded that this shows there is no such thing as motion; but there are other ways of dealing with the paradox.

Philosophy from Broadview Press:

J.E. Bickenbach
Canadian Cases in the Philosophy of Law
publishing 1991

John Burbidge
Within Reason: A Guide to Non-Deductive Reasoning
"an important and unique contribution...an excellent text"
Joseph C. Flay, Penn State University
"a most impressive text...at last: a thoughtful effort to approach reasoning
as it actually occurs in day-to-day contexts"
Robert Switzer, Queen's University

David Gallop, editor and translator
Aristotle on Sleep and Dreams
publishing 1991

Trudy Govier
God, The Devil and the Perfect Pizza
"a delightful book...encourages students to become involved in philosophy"
Prof. J. Mayer, Brock University

Michael Neuman
What's Left: Radical Politics and the Radical Psyche
"an extremely funny writer armed with a serious critique"
The Globe and Mail

Mervyn Sprung
The Magic of Unknowing: An East-West Soliloquy
"an exceptionally well-written book, on a subject of fundamental
importance"
Canadian Philosophical Reviews

Jacques D'Hondt
Hegel in His Time
"the first book we ought to read about Hegel"
H.S. Harris, author of Hegel's Development

John Thomas & Wilfrid Waluchow
Well and Good: Case Studies in Biomedical Ethics
"superb...wide in scope but concrete in the way it grapples with these
problems"
Daniel Callahan, Hastings Center

Michael Yeo
Concepts and Cases in Nursing Ethics
publishing 1991

Printed in Canada